THE TALES OF DISCO CHOOK

A Memoir

TAN IZZY

First published by Busybird Publishing 2020

Copyright © 2020 Tan Izzy

ISBN

978-1-922465-16-0 (paperback)

978-1-922465-17-7 (ebook)

The quoted text in the chapter titled 'Coffee and chats' is taken from Stacey Demarco, The Coffee Oracle: Discover your Future and Fortune in a Coffee Cup, Hay House Australia, 2008, p 210. The novel A Little Life mentioned in the chapter titled 'Adventures' is by Hanya Yanagihara.

Cover image and design: Dana Ivosevich, www.soulfulheart.yoga

Editor: Desanka Vukelich

Layout and typesetting: Busybird Publishing

busybird
publishing

Busybird Publishing
2/118 Para Road
Montmorency, Victoria
Australia 3094
www.busybird.com.au

Dedicated to
the Original
Disco Chook.

Mum, I will
always love you
around the world
and back again.

Tunny x

THE TALES OF DISCO CHOOK
A MEMOIR BY TAN IZZY

DISCO CHOOK AND CO.

Disco Chook was the nickname given to my mum in the '70s, the era of disco. Her last name sounds like Chook, so she was dubbed the Disco Chook or Chookie by her friends and family on the Northern Beaches of Sydney where she grew up.

I have an iconic photo of my mum. She is in a bar with her cousin wearing a Ringer Tee that's white with the words DISCO CHOOK in red velour sewn across the front. She made it herself. Mum used to make a lot of her clothes and this is by far one of my favourite photos of her.

I have always loved this nickname and made Mum tell me the story behind it countless times, so I have adopted it now to tell my story.

PROLOGUE

I have always wanted to write a book on my life. A true story. One that is heartfelt and genuine, but also awkwardly inappropriate at times.

My story will hopefully empower others to keep their head up high, even though life sometimes deals us some wild cards. Sometimes you've got to ride out a bad hand to get to the good stuff.

I want this book to entertain, and brighten your day, but I also want it to be real and raw when it needs to be, as life is not always fun and games. Well, so far I have had my fair share of both. Life is what you make it, you learn from your mistakes, but it's important to have these experiences, as they shape the story of who you really are.

Writing a book was always something I said I would do, but life gets busy and we run out of time for things we should make time for. Step one is always the hardest but it is also the necessary one, so here goes.

It was a rough start to 2020. Raging fires charred our beloved sunburnt country, Mother Nature then did a flip and along came flash-flooding. Then a global pandemic caused the world to stop, check in with what really matters and self-isolate to curb the spread of the virus, which is ongoing around the world as I write.

But to top off a cracking start to the year was the real fucking cherry on top. I lost my mum after her courageous six-year battle with breast cancer. My mum, who was my hero, but also my best friend.

Writing is a way to help clear my head, and over the last few months with Mum, we got in the habit of reflecting on all the amazing times we had together, telling stories, reminiscing about the good, the bad and the crazy.

I thought you had to be famous to write a story on your life. I may not be famous, but that's not a reason to stop me from sharing these stories.

This book is about the adventure that has been my life so far, from growing up on a farm in a surf town on the Central Coast of New South Wales, then moving to Melbourne in my early twenties.

I am a Virgo, a middle child and an absolute tomboy at heart. I love to socialise and those that know me know my friends and family mean the world to me. I have a loving husband who is so supportive and accepts me for the real me.

There have been influential people in my life that have been role models and taught me the importance of values and ethics, not to mention how to socialise like an absolute Queen.

All these moments have shaped who I am today, all these things have added to the story of my life. Geez, it's been an interesting ride so far.

So please, kick back, grab a beer and enjoy the tales of Disco Chook.

SECOND GEN.

I have tanned skin and I am tall, 6'1", which sure is tall for a girl, but that would be thanks to my Serbian genes. My tall frame only took me 30 years to grow into and appreciate.

I know some of you are thinking you would kill to be tall! Really? So tall that all pants are capri pants, sleeves never quite reach your wrists – three-quarter length is trendy right? – that for every school photo, you're in the middle back row with the boys and every crush you ever had was a good foot shorter than you? But yeah, now I love it; you've got to love and accept who you are if you want anyone else to.

My family is from a Serbian background, but we grew up very Aussie. The beach, sport and BBQs have become some of my best memories.

Hot summer days we spent at the beach. My dad who back in the day refused, and I mean refused, to wear boardshorts and only wore Speedos as that's how they did it when he was a lifeguard growing up. Cringe! My siblings and I attempting to bodyboard and having an absolute blast as we did. I was the pipsqueak of the family and had a fear of drowning. Dad always seemed so big and strong, nothing scared him. He would tell me to hold on tight and drag me out to the back of big waves. He used to say, 'Tunny, hold your breath, we are going under this next one.'

I would be beside myself with fear thinking, 'This is it. I am a goner! Farewell, world!' but of course I held my breath like my dad instructed and we would make it out alive to the other side.

See, the way you did it, the smart way which you learn as a kid, is to get out far, past where the waves are breaking, so you can get a really big wave that hasn't even started to form yet. You start paddling and kicking like there is no tomorrow and you catch it before it breaks. Always helped that I had my huge 6'4" dad to give me that extra power I needed to catch it all the way to the shoreline. I would jump up with a huge grin on my face, thinking, 'Look out! Here comes the Coast's latest and greatest pipe master!' and then we would do it all over again.

Back in the early days, we would spend the whole day at the beach, slip, slop, slap, catching up with other families and friends, building epic sandcastles, playing French cricket, getting an ice-cream and just enjoying moments that when you think about them take you back straight away.

When it was time to go home, the sky would be changing colour and a storm would be coming in. The clouds would get darker and darker, the wind would pick up and it was time to run back and pile into our RS2000 Ford Escort, an absolute beauty of a two-door car. World's tallest family getting into the world's smallest car.

We were lucky as we had the best of both worlds being Aussie and Serb.

We celebrate our Slava each year, which is a family day or Patron Saint's Day. This comes from back in the day when you couldn't afford to have multiple birthdays for all your children, so you celebrated them all at once on your Slava. We also did double Christmases and Easters. Serbian Orthodox people go by the Julian calendar for Christian events, so Christmas is celebrated on 7 January, and Easter is at different times each year, often not on the same date as on our everyday Gregorian calendars. As a child that was a blessing – double the fun, not to mention chocolate and gifts, so it's double the celebrations. It's a tradition we still continue in our family.

We were always proud to be both Serbian and Australian. Our grandparents on both sides taught us about our family history. They explained from a young age that family is everything, and you always needed to be proud of where you came from.

Our grandparents chose to come to Australia to have a better life for the generations to come. My Deda Mico, my dad's dad, always said Australia was God's country! Nothing was better than Australia. He told us that he was proud of living here, but that it's important to know your heritage. He made it clear even as children that we should be proud to live in such a beautiful country. He would say this while wearing a white Bonds singlet and drinking a VB, so it seemed he really adapted to the lifestyle here.

When Deda Mico came over to Australia by boat, his wife, my Baba Pera, was pregnant with my dad. My grandparents had already had their two other children, my aunties.

Aunty Jana we called Keka. Tetka is the Serbian word for aunty, but when my sister was younger she couldn't pronounce Tetka. Keka loved her new nickname, given to her by her first niece, so it stuck, and we think it sounds cooler anyway. Keka is the matriarch of the family, she's the oldest and I like to think wisest of my dad's siblings. She is tough, but has a soft spot for animals, and loves trivia and sweets. You could win Keka with any of the above. Keka never had children of her own, but loves kids, especially when they're little. As we've got older, our relationship with Keka has developed. You always know what you're going to get with her, there is no bullshit – she tells it how it is, and to have an aunty or uncle like that is just so refreshing.

Aunty Jill is the traveller of the family. She has maybe spent more time travelling than she has being in one spot. She was a bit of a hippy going by pictures of her back in the day. Long dark hair and tanned skin.

Mico and Pera met during the second world war, and married while they were living in a displaced persons camp in southern Italy. Their boat trip to Australia was long and unpleasant. Baba was very sick with motion sickness as well as morning sickness. There was no fresh fruit or vegetables, a lot of people got very ill on the boat as it wasn't the cleanest, and there were a lot of people crammed into small spaces. My Deda would come up to the top deck to take his two little girls to the bathroom.

I remember a story about someone giving him an orange, what a nice gesture it was. He gave that orange to my Baba and the aroma of it helped calm her seasickness down. He said he knew from that moment he'd made the right decision to bring his family to Australia.

My mother's parents met after the war once they had already arrived. Mum's father, Danilo, was working in Adelaide. One year, he spent Christmas in Sydney where he met my grandma, my Baba Mirjana, and fell in love with her instantly. He moved to Sydney just over a month later to marry her. Mirjana looked just like a film star, she was tall, elegant and always dressed glamorously. Danilo was a very charming and handsome man and well educated. Growing up as the son of a judge, they even had servants in the house, but after the war, everything changed.

My grandparents on both sides couldn't be more different from each other, chalk and cheese, but they were very good friends and solid role models to their grandkids. They always taught us about the world, our heritage and that you had to work hard for what you wanted. They all came to a new country and had to start afresh after a devastating war. It's amazing they even survived to tell their story. Our grandparents had to build themselves from the ground up without even speaking the language. It's just incredible what they accomplished. It makes me feel so proud and has taught me to be thankful for what I have in my life, not worry about what I don't have.

Growing up on the Central Coast, we were about as woggy as it got. Our primary school was quite small in comparison to some, about 200 kids or so from Kindergarten to Year 6. There was an Italian family, a Greek family and us – that covered all the Europeans.

It was a close community, you felt safe and people looked out for one another. We would ride our bikes to school, all three of us kids in a line riding our BMXs three kilometres each way. We kept active and fit and loved the freedom that came with having a bike. If you wanted to stop at the corner store for some lollies after school you could, if you wanted to ride down along the drain pipes you would.

We grew up with a lot of great friends and felt like we were accepted with most of the kids at school. Days were filled with sports like soccer or handball. The handball championships were a big event at school and everyone would get involved, didn't matter if you were hopeless, you would always give it a go. I on the other hand got my excellent ball skills from my mother, so gave the kids a run for their money in trying to take out the position of King. You needed to hold onto the title of King as long as you could. If the bell rang, then you were safe and owned the title for another day.

There were still dickheads at the school, unfortunately, just like in the real world. It is almost like you need them around when you're young to prepare yourself for life with them. One day when I was running late for school Mum drove me down in the Escort. It was the early '90s so my mum was most definitely rocking a perm. She also loved to wear headscarfs; they became a trademark look for her.

On our way to school, as it was a small town, Mum pulled over to ask a boy several years older than me if he would like a lift as it was obvious he was running late for class too. Mum thought it was a nice gesture seeing we were heading there anyway.

He said 'No!'

That was the end of that, or so we thought. Turns out this peanut, who at the time would have been about 12 years old, as I was maybe eight, told his mates at school that my mum was trying to kidnap him. Well, did I cop it at school. They made fun of me every day for the rest of that year, until they graduated and thankfully pissed off.

At the time, to make matters worse, oh, and I cringe thinking about this, I had a black front tooth. When I was younger, I'd slipped and hit my baby front tooth so hard on the porcelain bathtub that I actually caused nerve damage. A few weeks later the tooth went black, and it just became something I learnt to live with until it finally decided to fall out – years later! These morons made fun of not only my mum but my black tooth. Make fun of my black tooth all you want, but please leave my mum and her cute headscarfs and friendly manner out of this!

After those jerks left school, I vowed to never let a bully treat me or anyone else like that again, not on my watch. As I got older I was at least a head taller than all the guys. Me being a giant, I held my own in the playground, no problem. I wouldn't say I am a violent person, quite the opposite really, but during those years in primary I sure did get in my fair share of fights.

They were always fights where I was protecting someone who was getting picked on (it's a trait and I still have it to this day) and they were always with a boy. Not just any boy but a fucking bully.

One year I was buddy to a new kid, someone I had to take around the school and make feel comfortable for the start of the new year. Her name was Emma. She was a few years younger than me and I didn't know her full backstory, but from what I had gathered, her parents had died in a car crash when she was very young. She was a real introvert and her grandparents took her to school every day. Em was a super sweet girl and very shy.

One day, I overheard a boy named Cullen being a real dick to her. I remember standing up to him and I also remember getting punched in the eye.

When I said I got in fights, well, they were more chasing each other and grabbing onto each other's uniforms and a bit of pushing around. I had never actually been punched in the face before, and what do you think I did? Well, I cried like a girl who had been punched in the face by a boy. Thankfully I can say that was the only time it's happened to me and next time I will learn to duck.

Bloke didn't even get expelled, just suspended, and I got a firm talking to by the principal about how it wasn't my job to get involved and fight other people's battles, but little did she know I had already made a promise to myself, and that sure as hell wasn't going to change for one black eye.

FARM LIFE

Growing up on the Central Coast, life was fun, it was easy, and we didn't have to lock our doors. We were lucky, it was a pretty safe environment.

We made up our own games, we'd climb into the haystack and pea-shoot the chickens with chicken feed, we had a billycart and of course a treehouse which was pretty basic. It had four wooden planks and we would sit on this huge branch and eat and chat about life and our next adventure would ensue.

We were a bunch of ratbags, but with excellent manners and respect for our elders.

I grew up the middle child of three kids. My brother Michael is switched on, very adventurous and smart as fuck. My sister Dana has a heart of gold, she's softly spoken and the sensitive one of us. A free spirit and a hippy to an extent, minus the weed. Sometimes I feel she would make more sense if she did smoke a joint every now and then. I was somewhere in between, definitely the bossy one and maybe even the attention-seeker, but I was also the mother hen and I liked trying to be one of the grown-ups – this is where I got my love of socialising at a very young age from.

My mum was a real dork but also a real classy lady. To me she is a style icon, red lipstick, red nails to match, she was always making us kids laugh and being a fantastic mum! She was a pillar of strength and the courage she taught us kids by example is something else that made us the people we are today, and she really did it all on her own.

My dad is a big bloke famous for being tall and having grey hair, likes to think of himself as a bit of a silver fox. He is a big talker, a dreamer with a big heart but it's usually in the wrong place so unfortunately it gets him in a lot of strife.

Dad also must have got his guidebook on how to be a great role model in the cereal box because the bloke has zero idea and has made some very poor decisions that have haunted the family for most of our lives.

I loved my family growing up, and I didn't know we were a tad dysfunctional. It's only when I reflect now I think, oh yeah, my dad was always doing something very dodgy.

As a young girl, I rarely recall my dad having a steady job. I know he had one at some stage, but I can't pinpoint that time in my life.

My mum had always been the breadwinner. I have no idea how she managed that when we were very young. She cleaned houses for a living and as we got older we would laugh that she used to dress with an apron as though she were a French maid. Then later Mum worked part time in a department store. She did the best with what she had, and that worked for us kids.

The only family holiday we ever had was on Flybuys points to Port Stephens and we stayed for two nights. At a Best Western of all places. No offence to Best Western, but to this day I avoid them if I can. On this first family holiday with all five of us, the highlight was when we all went on a dolphin boat cruise called the Tamboi Queen. We got to sit in the nets in the water and actually almost swim with dolphins. It was an incredible experience. Years later I worked out Mum's good friend Nada and her husband at the time owned the tour company and that's how we got the hook-up. But it all worked out and we loved it. As a kid on a holiday who just got to see dolphins for the first time, and so close up, I was living my best tween life. Other activities included playing tennis at the hotel and stopping at Maccas on the way home, but as far as holidays went, that was our first and last as the five of us.

We lived on a 26-acre property with a dam and our house was a pretty small three-bedroom cottage, but was filled with food, love and laughs most of the time. It was our home and we loved and respected it.

We had an Odyssey, a 4-wheel beach buggy to drive around the property. We also had a few bush bashers as that's what farm life is all about.

Dad put a lock on the beach buggy, so it couldn't go much faster than about 20 km/hour because when my brother was four years old he was allowed to drive it on his own, much to my mother's shock when she asked Dad who was driving the buggy down the back, and he replied, 'Michael is'.

This same buggy also needed roll bars put on by Dad, as my Uncle Jimmy rolled it.

One memory is when we were with our Kumovi, which means your God family in Serbian. Kumovi is plural, and refers not only to your godparents, but the family as a whole. The godmother is your Kuma and the godfather is your Kum. It is quite common for the Kum to be the best man at your wedding, as my dad was for my godfather. Forever your families are classed as Kumovi. It is a close relationship, as close as being related by blood to us. We were so close to these guys growing up, and nothing has changed over the years; if anything, we've grown even closer as time has gone by.

When they were over one day, we wanted to see how many we could fit in the beach buggy. We all crammed in, three kids and three teenagers. We came back with scratches and bruises as the older boys steered it along a dirt track way down the back of the property. Even if you wanted to get off, you couldn't – you had to hold on for dear life and hope you made it back to the house in one piece. What a sight we must have been, just bodies and limbs, all holding on by an arm, a leg or perched on someone's lap.

We had a mixture of pets, including a German Shepherd named Bazza who was a sweetheart. We had a few German Shepherds over the years. That was the only breed of dog Dad would approve of, as when he was a small boy, he lived on a property as well and nearly drowned one day playing in the dam. Their family dog saved him. It's a pretty good reason to be loyal to a breed of dog. We also had rabbits, a Shetland pony, cattle and chickens. We even had a giant glasshouse where Deda grew vegetables such as cucumbers and tomatoes.

People also kept their horses at our property and Dad would take a slab of beer as payment. This is how us kids learnt to ride a horse. They would teach us and take us for a ride when they were over on days when we got lucky. As a kid this was an amazing opportunity.

I was always a scaredy-cat but loved the idea of adventure, sometimes more than the adventure itself. Although after my brother had an incident riding a horse, I never wanted to ride one again and haven't to this day. Somehow while going for a ride when he was quite young, maybe seven years old, the horse got spooked and then Bazza started chasing it. The horse took off, then my dad took off. My brother had fallen off and somehow got his leg stuck in the stirrup.

The vision I have is of Mum chasing Dad, who is chasing the dog who is chasing the horse, and my brother hanging down off the horse by his leg. I still have no idea how Michael didn't get harpooned by a tree as he got dragged along the rugged terrain.

Crisis averted, he was fine, not really even a scratch on him. The dog got a belting, the horse was okay and Dad would also have got a belting from Mum for letting my seven-year-old brother with zero riding experience ride a horse unsupervised with no helmet.

On the farm I also had to share a room with my sister in the early years which was covered in the latest posters from *Dolly* magazine, with the likes of Dylan from *Beverly Hills, 90210* and Freddie Prinze, Jr coating our walls. I absolutely hated sharing a room with Dana. We were and still are the two most different human beings on the planet. Maybe on a good week we might have got along one day out of the seven. We would argue over the dumbest shit, like my sister would never share her Easter eggs and I would always offer mine to enjoy with the family. She would hide things and save them and I was a one-for-all-and-all-for-one kind of girl.

Once we had a big blue over who knows what, something silly no doubt, so we split the room in two. We put a strip of packing tape right through the centre of the room, which meant one had to use the window to leave the room rather than the door.

My dad is a big dreamer. He thought there was always a quick way to get rich. This never worked, you see. He still tries this style of income, when he just needs to get a job like the rest of society.

He was always wheeling and dealing ideas with his 'business' mates. There was on average four to six people that came to our house to hang out. As we had a farm, there was plenty of room. I mastered the art of making coffee from the age of about eight as that's all they seemed to do: drink coffee and talk. Dad took his coffee with full cream milk and sugar, and he had about six to eight a day, no lunch, just about two litres of milk through the day in all those coffees. This was about the time my dad developed a bit of a milk gut. Rather than from beer, it was from drinking way too much full cream milk. That can't be a healthy diet for anyone. All these blokes hanging out at ours was strange. I guess it would've been normal if they all had jobs, but none of them did. My dad is a nice guy, he attracts the strays.

I worked out real quick, that's how my dad's Stray Cat Club worked. 'Oh, you don't have a job and you want to work on your car and drink Nescafe instant coffee all day? Sure, come on over!'

Seems like a great idea to get a business venture off the ground, right? Work, who needs that? Meanwhile Mum is bringing home the bacon, supplying litres of milk on tap for the coffee club on a part-time salary for a family of five. Epic, hey? Foolproof plan, Dad.

In later years, this was somewhat helpful when my Gemini blew a head gasket, and I had a few blokes to do the labour if I just continued to bring them Blend 43s and put up with not one but four men telling me Dad jokes.

But like my dad's stray friends that he collected over time, we also seemed to collect stray animals at our house. We had a goat that turned up one day. It just appeared in the paddock, and it was quite nimble at getting from one side of the fence to the other. Sometimes it hung out with the cattle, sometimes it spent time near the clothesline. It even disappeared for a few weeks once and then came back with a horn missing. It was a naughty billy goat, that's for sure, but he didn't seem to bother us too much.

I also had some pet ducks a friend dropped over one day. There was a knock at the door and I looked down to see a cardboard box with three little ducklings inside. I adored them from the moment I laid eyes on them. I spent so much time with them. As ducklings, they followed me around in a line. My Baba popped over one day to tell me they would be perfect for eating when they were bigger. I was shocked. 'Baba, you can't eat my ducks!' Once they got big enough, we let them move from the rabbits' cage they had been living in to the chicken coop. I went down to visit them the next day and my dad told me that they must've flown away or moved to another dam as they were never seen again. We all know this was not true. Farm life, hey?

RIP Peanut, Cashew and Nutty, I will always hold a spot for you in my heart.

When I was a kid I really wanted a kitten, I wanted one so bad and would request one for my birthday and Christmas religiously every year. Mum said she would think about it, but Dad would say flat-out no. Well one day Dad was working for someone doing a delivery, he used to drive this old Chevy ute. He was strapping down the boxes with an occy strap, across his ute sideways. Now if you are unaware of what an occy strap is, it is an elastic bit of rubber covered in fabric with a metal hook at each end. This day Dad was doing the same thing he had done hundreds of times before, but he got unlucky.

He attached it to one side and went to strap it across the load, but it mustn't have been locked in properly, as when he was trying to fasten the other hook, with force, it whipped across the back and the hook went straight into Dad's eye, well his cornea, to be exact. Later we learnt the best thing to do is leave it, so you don't do more damage ripping it out. Dad being Dad pulled it out and drove himself to hospital. He did end up doing more damage that way, he had to have an operation and stay almost a week. Poor Dad! A silver lining to this story is while Dad was in hospital, it was the perfect opportunity to get the pet kitten I had wanted so badly. Mum and I found him, a ginger tom cat I named Mickey. He was the best, so cute with a strangely smaller head than the rest of his body, but I loved him so. Dad finally got home from hospital and it was time to let him know about our newest housemate, Mickey the cat! Dad, feeling pretty sorry for himself, loved Mickey instantly. He had a little mate to cuddle up to on the lounge, while his eye was healing and he was licking his own wounds. Dad's eye ended up with 90 percent perfect vision again. The only part that really changed was for a period of six months, he had to wear an eyepatch, so not only was my dad a tall silver fox, now he was a pirate, too.

Bazza, our German Shepherd, loved Mickey the cat. They were little partners in crime running amok around the farm. Sunbaking together, you would always find them side by side, a bit like Milo and Otis, except one was a giant dog. Sadly, when Bazza passed away, it really upset us kids, he was the first death we had in the family and such a good family dog. Leading up to his death, he had this tendency to go under the house. He would always go to this one spot and lie there. Dad explained Bazza knew he was dying and some dogs liked to do it that way. We knew he was older and had bad arthritis which is something that breed of dog can get quite badly. One day he didn't come back out from under the house. He was gone and the whole family was devastated. Mickey took it the hardest, he longed to have his mate back. He was sulking and mourning the death of Bazza like we all were but you could tell Mickey was just heartbroken. He started going under the house, to the spot Bazza died in. If we couldn't find him, we knew that's where he would be, he would sit in the same patch of dirt and spend the whole day there in sorrow.

A few weeks later the strangest thing happened. Dana and I were in our room, it was almost bedtime and we were settling in for the evening. We got distracted by a sound, a faint noise, which at first we thought was coming from our wardrobe. We called out for Dad to come and inspect it and make sure it was safe to go to bed. We did not want to get attacked by a monster from the cupboard – I had read enough *Goosebumps* books to know what happens next.

Dad came in and realised there was indeed a noise, but it was coming from under the floorboards, not from our room. Dad went outside to investigate with his big mag flashlight. He had to go under the house as that is where the strange sound was coming from.

We were nervous waiting to see what he'd discover. A short time later, in walks Dad with a smile and something in his hands, but we couldn't quite make out what it was. It was small and sounded like it was purring!

It was a kitten, a tiny, scrawny purring kitten. She was adorable! Dad put her down and she went sliding across the floorboards to Mickey's cat food and started hoovering it down. The poor thing was starving, who knows when she'd had her last meal. Her purr was so loud we called her Rumble as it felt like that's what the floorboards were doing.

Straightaway us girls called out, 'Can we keep her, Dad?' Dad rolled his eyes. 'We'll discuss it in the morning.'

Of course we kept her, she was a little blessing. We lived about a kilometre away from the next property, so she had gone on quite a hike to get to us.

We had to keep her, it was meant to be. The strange part was, Dad found her in the exact same spot where Bazza had died.

TOMBOY AT SCHOOL CAMP

As I mentioned, I was a tomboy, and boy oh boy, I do not lie.

My uniform was a backwards cap – in the early years I would go for a Finch or a Rusty, in the later years Chicago Bulls, my favourite basketball team, so that's what I rocked – and I wore shorts everywhere. I hated wearing dresses. The only time I wore a dress in my younger days was when us kids had to go to church for Orthodox Christmas or Easter, or when we had a wedding to attend. Mum would have us decked out thanks to her mostly excellent but sometimes questionable taste from the latest Country Road catalogue.

But yes, shorts, an oversized Tee and backwards cap was my jam. I got mistaken that many times for a boy, Mum started asking me to not have my hair in a pony all the time.

But she also never tried to change who I was. Both my parents accepted me for who I was.

I had plenty of girlfriends, but liked sport, so played a lot more with the boys.

Mum was asked by one of my teachers in primary school if there was something wrong with me, as I spent so much time with the boys. Mum came to my defence. She had no problem with it, having grown up with brothers and male cousins too. This was not an issue in our house, and so what if I did? It's insane to think this teacher suggested my parents have me speak to someone about my behaviour. Imagine in this day and age if a teacher suggested that? The bird obviously had no idea how to be a good supportive teacher.

I also had an issue with the school uniform, as it was a tunic dress, and being super tall and lanky at a young age, the dress was short, and I bloody hated wearing it. I used to wear bike shorts underneath it as when I was playing soccer, I didn't want the boys to see my undies. I might have been a tomboy, but I had self-respect and standards.

Because I was so thin, a size up would swim on me, so Mum (legend) made shorts out of the same fabric which I would wear with our Friday sports T-shirt. By the time I finished primary school lo and behold the uniform got changed to that for everyone.

In Year 5, there was a school camp.

Even though I was tall for my age and stood up to bullies, I was the biggest wimp when it came time to go on this camp. I hated it so much, I hated the idea of leaving my mum at home.

As a kid, even though I shared a room with my sister, I used to get super scared at night and would try run into Mum and Dad's bed every night to snuggle in. It got so bad and I used to wake them so much, Mum got in the habit of making up a little bed next to her side of the bed, so I could camp out on the floor with a pillow and blanket.

This feeling of homesickness is the worst. As I write, my mother has just passed away after a battle with breast cancer, and even though I will get into it later, the way I am describing my grief now is a feeling of homesickness, that feeling where you long to see your mum, and nothing will be okay again till you do. You have that feeling in the base of your guts that something bad will happen and the only thing that will make it go away is that feeling of knowing you are home and will see your mum again.

But, back to school camp. I used to hate it but Mum would make me go as she knew I would have so much fun once that feeling passed. And she was right, of course she was right, mums know everything. She also used to leave super cute notes in my bag like:

> Mummy loves you! xx
> Don't forget to brush your teeth xx
> See you in a few days, Tunny xx
> Love you round the world and back again xx

which is an adorable habit I picked up from her and now my husband gets to enjoy cute secret notes.

For this year's school camp we were going to Canberra, and Mum had got me a brand-new matching Adidas tracksuit. I remember thinking, 'I look cool as fuck!' I think Mum bought it as bribery so I would go on the camp, so with that and a backpack filled with Gummy bears and my Walkman, I was on my way. Well, so I thought. When I got on the bus I panicked and got off crying. Mum gave me the biggest hug and said if I was still this upset when I got to Canberra, she would come and pick me up. This calmed me down, as I knew Mum wouldn't lie and had my best interests at heart. So I did what I had to do, I put on my big-girl pants which were in the form of a sweet new tracksuit and got on the bus, straight to the backseat. I headed to where my friends had saved me a spot where the cool kids sit. Even though I was just crying to my mum like a big baby and I waved at her through the tears, I had my friends around me and knew it was going to be okay, and it was.

Well, it was almost all okay. During the day, we went to Parliament House and a science museum and for one of the night activities, we were meant to go to Telecom Tower. Now known as Telstra Tower, there's a lookout that is situated at the summit of Black Mountain. Two classmates and I got ready early as we wanted to try get the backseat, so we stepped outside our room to wait near the bus. We got yelled at by a teacher and told to wait in our rooms. This teacher, who nobody really liked, I think at the time was going through a divorce and became a really sour and mean woman to be around.

We went to our rooms and waited, killing time with some chocolate bars, and waited and waited and waited some more. We didn't hear a sound and it was strange, as the bus was meant to be leaving shortly. Fed up and bored, we stepped outside and noticed that the bus had left with all 70 kids and forgotten us.

Now, we were about 11 years old, no mobile phone, our hotel was pretty much on the side of a freeway. How the fuck do teachers forget the tallest girl in the year with her two shortest friends?

We stood out like a sore thumb! The hotel, more like a motel, was connected to a lobby with a restaurant area. We went and asked the people working there if they knew what we should do. They told us to go to our room, lock the door and not open it for anyone. Cheers mate, solid advice!

So, we did, and a good three hours later there was a thump at our door. It was our two teachers with their tails between their legs apologising for forgetting us.

We were young, but we weren't dumb. We knew full well they realised they'd forgotten us and didn't turn the bus around. For the rest of the camp we got the backseat and served first every time.

They tried to sweep it under the rug and pleaded with us not to tell our parents, but times were a bit different back then. Our parents had firm words to them and the whole thing was forgotten. If anything, it's become a private joke between us about the time we got stranded at the side of a freeway when the bus left us on school camp.

CARTRAK

As mentioned, my dad did not like to go out to work. You can call it anything you want, but he'd prefer working his arse off all day for nothing than have a 9–5 job and actually earn an income for the family.

One of my dad's latest and greatest business ventures was one his 'friend' Gary tried to lure him into, and if they did it properly, it might have actually worked.

It was about 1995, and the idea was to have a device on your car that tracked it by satellite, so if it was stolen, they could track it, hence, Cartrak.

Incidentally, while Dad was trying to get into the preventative car theft business, one day, Mum's RS2000 was stolen while she was at work. It actually got given back to her because the cops found my sister's school diary in the car with her full name and address in it. Lucky, as we loved that car! But after this, Dad made Mum chain up the steering wheel with a thick chain thrown over the wheel and around the brake pedal, held together with a giant padlock. So rather than use a steering wheel lock like all our friends' parents, here's Mum having to go about locking up this massive chain every day because Dad was always one step ahead. Or so he told us.

Anyway, this phase of Cartrak consisted of my dad going to 'the office' every day, where, you know the deal by now, he drank a lot of instant coffee.

Now some of the roadblocks were: (a) neither he nor Gary had the money to kick-start this idea, and (b) neither had common sense when it came to actually putting their idea into action. An idea is great but you need the rest to fall into place to make that idea come alive. To be fair, I do recall Dad driving to Sydney a lot for meetings to try secure finance to get it off the ground.

I vividly recall another part of this tracking system needed a big satellite. There was plenty of room to put one on our property. It was mostly open space, but there were also parts hidden down the back among the pine trees. But of course it would make sense to have it in the middle of the open bit of land.

So there's my dad's huge manmade metal satellite sitting there for all the world to see. It had no wires and wasn't connected by any power or electricity, so I am really not sure what the purpose was, but like all the ideas in the past, this idea never took off and things didn't work out. This was another one to add to the list, but now we had a giant souvenir on our property to yet again remind us that not only did Dad live on another planet, but now neighbours driving past would think that his family did too, and we all wanted to reconnect with them in outer space via a satellite.

LARRY AND BOB

'Dad, why are there two men in caravans camping down the back?'
I asked one day.

'Oh, that's just Larry and Bob. They needed a place to stay,' Dad
answered.

One day we came home from school to understand Larry and
Bob had moved into caravans on our property, using our electricity,
and would be joining us for dinner every night.

Bob cooked so I guess that was all right, right? No, it wasn't all
right, it was fucking odd.

Larry was an IT wizard who needed a place to stay after a
company my dad wanted to start with him backfired, as in it never
got off the ground. Larry was divorced and liked to go on internet
chat rooms and chat to women. He also liked to walk around with
leg weights strapped to his ankles and do sit-ups.

Bob was an extremely obese man who liked to tell stories about
all the tail he got back in his younger years. And eat, wow could
he put away the food. Bob also had a very red face. (Think Santa
without the suit and much plumper.) Bob was also divorced, not
once but twice.

One night we were all sitting around in the carport at the outside
table, and Bob yet again had had too much wine to drink, and
managed to get stuck in one of the metal chairs that came with our
outdoor dining setting. He got stuck in or buckled the chair legs a
couple of times while he was living on the farm.

Don't get me wrong, they were nice enough blokes, easy to chat
to, and family dinners had grown from five sitting around the table
to seven, but the table didn't really fit that many to begin with, yet
so began our new cramped family dinners. Conversation flowed,
but after about nine months, after Mum had asked Dad numerous
times to tell them to leave, Mum had to finally do it. Dad explained

he couldn't as he was their friend. Mum told them, thanks guys, it's been fun but can you bugger off now, which they took as a clear sign, and off they went to park their caravans on someone else's yard. Onya, Mum!

A JAIL BIRD

You might think that would be the first and last time we had squatters on our property – Dad learnt his lesson and we lived happily ever after. Ha, oh boy, you are so very wrong.

This brings me to our latest instalment of Who Will Squat Next, and the winner was housemate Harley. Harley was a strange character. I first met Harley through his dad. We all went to Sydney one night during the Olympics; our fathers knew each other through 'work'.

At the time, my siblings and I were in high school; I was 13. Harley was a guy that ended up not just living in a tent on the farm, but on the bloody couch.

Things I learnt about Harley: That he was a jail bird, he had a rat's tail, was in his late twenties, and was not attractive in any way. It wasn't like we had this dreamboat living on our couch with rock-hard abs that was a spitting image of Ryan Phillipe. Nope. A jail bird with a rat's tail who was in love with my poor sister. He had a V8 Holden station wagon which he drove like a lunatic and sometimes picked us up from school in it instead of Dad. Harley liked the dark and seemed a bit damaged. He was always staring and he really had a creepy vibe about him.

He confessed his love for Dana one night after picking her up from a party which Dad was meant to do but sent Harley instead.

I believe Harley told her something along the lines of 'I would kill for you'. Oh dear god. My poor sister. Again, Dad couldn't kick him off our lounge, so after six weeks, and some very strange confessions of love to my sister once again, Mum had to ask him politely to please get the hell out of our house and leave my sister alone. The bloke who came with no bags, just two T-shirts, had really overstayed his welcome.

At the same time, for some reason my dad had swapped my mum's new car, our family Commodore, with Harley's father's car. We had no idea why but Dad just said it was to help a friend out. So here's Mum driving to work, back and forth and all around with a car that supposedly had a hit on it! I kid you not. But Dad explained it was fine as they lived in Sydney, and Mum was safe on the Coast. To clarify, this is only about a hundred-kilometre distance. Fuck, seriously Dad. We never knew why but once we found out the truth, the cars were swapped back. Just another genius idea of Dad's to put his family first, I guess.

VEGETABLES HAVE FEELINGS TOO

Growing up I was lucky enough to have all four grandparents. Sadly, that is not the case now, I have lost them all. RIP, Babas and Dedas. I will love them forever and they influenced me a lot growing up. Grandparents are just the best. They love you like no one else. Being European their main purpose in life was to feed and love us grandkids, and well, that was just perfect with us.

My dad's dad was forever at our house. He lived nearby, and spent every spare moment at our place looking after the cows or the chooks, feeding them and pretty much just walking around, in a hat, Bonds singlet, dress-suit pants and leather shoes. That was his look and if he didn't have his hat on, he had wild hair (what was left of it). I loved his look. He often had just come from the markets and smelled like vegetables. But I loved that smell on him.

We used to have a glasshouse, filled with vegetables to eat. It was massive and extremely hot in there during the day. On winter nights Deda would light a fire in a big 44-gallon drum to keep the cucumbers warm. He thought they could feel the cold and grew better when they were warm. On those nights when I went to the bathroom before bed, I'd see a faint glow in the distance where the light from the fire looked kind of like an angel in the glass of the window, but this one night it looked like the angel was on fire! Something wasn't right, so I ran and yelled 'Dad! Dad! The glasshouse is on fire!'

It sure was! The drum had somehow not worked as planned (as usually all unwatched uncovered fires go). Mum, Dad and my sister had to run and put it out while the two youngest had to stay inside. Lucky I noticed, as our Shetland pony was in his stable right next door. Not only would the cucumbers have been baked in the morning.

While on the topic of Deda and his crazy ideas, the cattle we had on the farm were not just to keep the grass down, but more so because my Deda loved them. We had from a couple to a dozen at different times. Another thing he and Dad were not great at was making fences good enough to keep them on our property. If there was a medal for which farm on the Central Coast could let their cows escape the most, Deda and Dad would have won them all. We would come home riding our bikes back from school and there would be Deda with his suit pants, dress shoes, hat and singlet walking across a pretty busy road where the speed limit was 80 km/hour, trying to call the cows to come back in. Cows however are not dogs; they don't come when you call to them, but we would somehow manage to herd them all back in. This was extremely frightening for me as I feared cows, horses and pretty much any herbivore that had teeth that large.

GETTING EVICTED

It was my 14th birthday, a day that should have been spent focusing on friends, cake and of course those important things like seeing if my crush would wish me a happy birthday.

Birthdays were a big deal at our house. They were special; it's where the family came together for a big celebration. There was always plenty of food and cold drinks, not to mention Baba's famous birthday cake. My grandma made the same birthday cake for every single person in the family, for every birthday every year, whether you were turning two or 42.

It was a coffee crème layered sponge cake, with choc chips around the outside and choc chips on top formed in the shape of the number of whatever age you were turning – her version of a tiramisu. You might be thinking, coffee cake, how delicious. But as a kid, I am not going to lie, we hated it! We wanted an ice-cream cake or a chocolate mud any day of the week. We didn't drink coffee; coffee was gross like cigarettes and adults kissing in public. But Baba made it without fail every year and all the adults loved it. Now I love coffee and have one every day – I would do absolutely anything for a slice of that cake and a coffee with my Baba now.

Speaking of cakes, another big hit in our family was the *Women's Weekly Children's Birthday Cake Book*. See, if you grew up in Australia in the '80s or '90s, you would be well aware of this iconic book. It had it all when it came to dazzling party guests with a birthday themed creation. From the princess's castle cake which was decorated in cream-covered waffle cones, candy bracelets and smarties, to racing cars that had liquorice wheels, and my personal favourite, the bunny, this book really had it all. Our parents would go all-out for our birthdays and host parties on the weekend. Mum never wanted any kids to miss out, so there were plenty of times we invited the whole class, 20–30 students, just so everyone could enjoy themselves. Mum would even dress up in a bow tie and black suit with white shirt, the peak of '80s fashion – a woman in a pants suit.

When it came to presents, we never felt we missed out. We would always have the latest and greatest, from books or board games to clothing, and our all-time favourite was the latest craze in sporting goods from baseball caps, skateboards, roller blades, to that one year I got a hockey set complete with goal posts and all. How active and hands-on you could be with your present was the ultimate test of how it measured up as the most kick-arse birthday yet.

On the odd occasion when we were really young, Mum would find $50 notes hidden in our nappies from Kumovi or older generation family friends. My siblings are both born in April, and I'm a Virgo all the way in September. As a kid I couldn't work out why everyone was coming to visit and Dana and Mike were getting gifts or blocks of Cadbury's chocolate (another classic gift) but not me. Mum got in the habit of giving me a bonus gift even if it was something as small as a teddy bear or colouring book, just so I didn't feel left out.

Birthdays were always good memories. I smile whenever I think of that time my Baba Mirjana got excited on the jelly shots at a birthday party. We caught her red-handed in the kitchen about six shots down. She said she hadn't had jelly for years, was it raspberry flavour? Yes, Baba, it's raspberry and *vodka* flavour.

My 14th birthday was a little different to all that. I was down at the bus stop waiting to say goodbye to my mates after class, getting in a final happy birthday hug or high five, when my sister came running across the road calling my name, 'Tania, Tania, we've got to go now!'

She looked very panicked for Dana, so I grabbed my school bag and ran to meet her.

While driving to our property she informed me that the Sheriff had come to our house that day and changed the locks and evicted us.

Pardon, the Sheriff? What was this, a Western movie? Who knew there was a Sheriff on the Central Coast and why the hell would they be bothering us on my birthday! Didn't he understand what an inconvenience this was? The reality of what was happening hadn't sunk in yet.

I was brought smack-bang back to reality when we were driving down the long driveway to our family home, and this time had to park around the back so our car was out of sight. We couldn't be busted as we weren't meant to be on the property. Sure, this was our house, our home, but now we were trespassing in the eyes of the state.

Dana explained Dad had left a window open in our room and we had to climb in and get a washing basket and fill it with clothes for ourselves, but we also had to go into Mum and Dad's room and pack some things for Mum, work clothes especially, for Mum. Mum was still at work and had no idea what had happened. We loaded up the washing basket and climbed back out the window, leaving it unlocked in case we needed to come back again over the next few days to collect more of our belongings.

That night we all went to our Baba and Deda's nearby. It was a three-bedroom house, but we had to make it work for the seven of us. I don't think I can recall my parents ever having spent the night there before, whereas us kids did all the time. We loved going there and watching *Sale of the Century* or *The Golden Girls* with Baba. We loved to spend time with our grandparents. This time however was different, this time Mum and Dad had a big blue. Dad, you see, forgot to mention to Mum that he'd had not one but three warning letters from the Sheriff regarding payment on the house being overdue.

See the backstory goes, my grandparents used to live there, but when my parents first moved to the Central Coast from Sydney, they did a house swap. It was quite common in a European way to get your inheritance early to set you up for life, so they swapped the deeds to the houses and we moved to the farm and Dad's parents moved to my parents' house.

This was a blessing because we got to see our Deda often. When he came every day to feed the cattle, he would also often drop off bread for us and something tasty to eat after school like apple or cheese strudel which Baba had cooked for us as a treat.

For my mum however, it was sometimes more of a pain, as every night, god bless my Deda, he would watch Mum cook dinner for the five of us – he would not eat or drink anything apart from a cold VB us kids would fetch for him – standing in the doorway. He would not actually come and sit inside the kitchen. No, he would stand in the doorway and comment on how Mum made dinner every single night. He would say, 'Pera wouldn't add that much salt, she would use more stock', and 'Now, that's too much pasta' etc. etc. Mum humoured him because she was well mannered and knew he was a good father-in-law and a good Deda to us kids, but thinking about that, geez what a punish that would have been.

And now we had been evicted and had to shack up with my grandparents. Dad said he would sort it out and it was just a small issue, but there we were, the seven of us; we lived in that three-bedroom house for three months in total. Mum went to work, Dad sat around and us kids went to school and so life went on. Somehow the bills got settled and finally we were able to get back into our family home again. I don't think I was ever so happy to share a room with my sister again, packing tape room divider and all.

THAT AWKWARD TIME FOR US ALL, ALSO KNOWN AS HIGH SCHOOL

In high school, it's an awkward time. You are trying to work out how to fit in and who you are. Do you straighten your hair with an actual iron like all the girls in class are doing? Yes, of course you do! Or how about when you go through that hair mousse phase, but instead of getting a natural beach wave, you end up looking more like an ethnic Slick Rick than a Boho Beach Babe. Is your skirt the right length, are you wearing the right brand of skate shoe? At the time I had Etnies, then Converse, so pretty on-trend I thought, but who knew? There were just so many rules.

If you are lucky, you have some primary school friends who continue through to the same high school as you. You meet a lot of new people; some you don't like and others you desperately want to like you. You know that saying, people are in your life for a reason, a season or a lifetime? I feel like this really started to make more sense during my teenage years. I realised I had no choice about some people being in my life, but some I thought the world of and I knew it was a pretty special thing.

I am not sure what schools are like these days, but the cool girls at our school were bitches. They would tease people, they were super vain, and they would throw you under a bus if it gave them a bit more street cred. Not ideal, but at the time you don't really get it as you think that's the group you should hang out with because they are the popular ones.

At a slumber party I went to with them once, I was getting teased for not having kissed a boy with tongue before. Yes, I knew it was a big deal but I didn't want to waste my first kiss on just anyone. I would call myself a romantic, these girls however were calling me frigid. Either way I wasn't ready, I was only 14, but I didn't need everyone to point and laugh. What's the big deal anyway? Dolly Doctor said it was like kissing a mango, surely it couldn't be that hard.

I did try for a moment in time to fit into this group, but it wasn't for me. There were too many bitches for my liking, and by the time I went through the years, these characters, well at my school at least, tended to drop out or leave. Hell, some were even knocked up with a kid before I had completed Year 12.

Influences play a big part on the person you want to be at this age. I was a little confused as I was running with the wrong crowd. One day I was sitting in Maths class next to a new girl. I hated that I had to sit next to this new bird, I was not keen on the idea at all and I was a bitch to her. She didn't do anything to me, other than maybe smile. I was flat-out rude back. Thankfully, I came to my senses and pulled my head in because she and I ended up becoming really good friends. She was one of my best mates through high school, we graduated together and we've moved through milestones in life, such as her wedding and first child. I'm so glad I was there for those moments. We went against the groove and started our own group based on real friendships, and others followed suit. It felt good, actually spending time with people because you liked them, not because it made you more popular. We all learn this on our own, some of it makes you cringe thinking back, but mostly it brings the smiles.

I was always talking in class. I think on every school report card from Kindergarten to Year 12 I had the same feedback:

> Tania would be better in class if she applied herself and stopped talking.
> Tania is a chatterbox in class and has the tendency to distract other children.
> Tania talks too much and if she made more of an effort to talk less and concentrate more her grades would improve.

I was average at school. If I liked the subject or tried, I was better than good. I picked subjects that I was into. Getting into university wasn't a focus for me. I did Art, Fashion Design, Hospitality and Retail as my electives. I weighed up skipping Maths to head to the beach or go for a drive. That was more important to me at the time. My parents were happy with that, as long as I tried with all the subjects I was interested in.

While I was still at high school, I was also studying Fashion at TAFE. You could combine the two back then. That was where I met one of my best friends, Elissa. We didn't know each other at all but worked out pretty quickly we had more than enough in common. Elissa had the biggest heart and the same hobbies – parties, fashion, boys, art, the beach – and the same values when it came to friendships and family. The very first time we planned to meet out of class was at a party. In the end, Elissa couldn't make it and had told her best mate Jemma to look out for a tall tanned girl named Tania. A girl came running up to me almost as soon as I entered the backyard. She told me she had a bag of goon and I was welcome to share it. I didn't know this girl from a bar of soap but instantly loved her. Jemma was funny and loud and we had the same shoes on – it was meant to be.

The best thing about meeting girls from another school was it opened more friendships. The girls had a solid group of wonderful friends, so with my squad and theirs, a beautiful new friendship group was formed. Jemma and Elissa went to a Catholic school not too far away from my high school. We used to try to sneak into each other's schools and once I almost made it into their class pretending I was a Swedish exchange student. The only issue being, I didn't look Swedish at all, nor could I speak it, and after that the jig was up pretty quickly, but it was all just innocent fun. Another good thing about knowing girls from another school was the more people you knew, the more parties you would get invited to, and at 17 this is what dreams were made of. Oh, and to those bitches in high school who teased me for not making out with a boy when I was 14, well, I well and truly made up for that when a few years later, I discovered a game called pash and dash on the foreshore of a Newcastle beach while celebrating New Year's Eve. Thanks to my new friends, there was no teasing, only laughs and encouragement, and I surely made up for some lost time over that summer.

GIRLS JUST WANT TO HAVE FUN

Elissa was the first of our friends who ended up relocating to Sydney. There were many adventures and lots of wild nights out with crazy tales of what we got up to.

One year we went to Mardi Gras. It was amazing; if you have never been, you should go! That night two women proposed to me, we danced in the streets and we got coated in glitter. It was the place to be. After the parade was wrapping up, we were headed to the Orient Hotel in The Rocks, but we couldn't make it in a cab because the roads were closed due to the floats. We had sore feet from the evening and we really couldn't make the walk, it had been a big session. No problem, we managed to flag down and hitch a ride with one of the trucks that had been connected to a float earlier and was now removing fences used in the event. We told the driver we needed a ride down to the Orient for a night of dancing and he told us to climb on in. Now thinking back as a wiser, older woman, this was probably one of the dumber things we had done. However, we got dropped right to the door. It was only when we were trying to climb down that the toothless truckie tried to not only get a kiss from me but Elissa as well for his troubles. To dodge the kiss, we both ended up flinging ourselves out of the truck and onto the footpath below. Granted, it wasn't our most glamorous entry, but we sure did dodge a bullet and knew it would make a good story later.

My first experience of going to a strip club was also in Sydney, when Kings Cross was the place to be. Bars, clubs and seedy strip joints, all the things an 18-year-old girl away in Sydney would dream of. One night Jemma and I were waiting for Elissa to finish work, so we were hanging out at the pub in Maroubra down the road from where she lived. Jemma and I had done a great job of chatting and drinking beers on this Tuesday night while we waited for Elissa to join us. It was a warm spring evening and we were in the perfect location. I was feeling pretty chuffed with myself having driven all the way down to Sydney, and now being at the pub with my girls, things were good!

I was feeling pretty grown up, and what is more grown up than getting intoxicated enough to think it's a good idea that us girls, as well as the new guy Elissa was seeing, should head out to the Cross to go to a strip club? I hadn't planned on going to a strip club, so I was wearing a strappy cream lace beach dress with a yellow cardigan. Cardigans were in at the time, but I don't think they were ever in enough for Porky's! Possibly judging by the name it wasn't the classiest joint. Entering the club, you walk down to a stage. The path leads down as you near the stage on an angle and I remember seeing plastic school chairs with the legs cut off, just like the blue ones you had in primary school. As I was strolling down, I slipped on something, god knows what, it was Porky's, after all, and I hit the deck! It was not quite the entry I expected to make in my yellow cardy. Who came to my rescue? Not one but two completely nude female strippers. They leaned down to pick me up and make sure I was okay. What I have learnt is, if you're going to do something, do it right. Go to Porky's for your first strip show, and fall on arrival only to be picked up physically by some nude strippers. They'll walk you to a seat so you can kick back and enjoy the show. The boy Elissa was seeing, let's call him Frenchie, didn't drink and also had never been to a strip club. Turns out after a few shots, the bloke's on stage whipping the strippers in a role-play; it really was a night of firsts.

Ah, they were the days. God I miss Kings Cross.

It was never a dull moment when Elissa, Jemma and I got together. On our first holiday together, Elissa's alter-ego Trudy came to life. Trudy thought she was a Brazilian dancer and liked to pash boys on the dance floor. Trudy sounds like fun in theory, but was wild, a little too wild. One of the last times I saw Trudy was in Bali, and let's just say the night ended with a bath and some nudity. That same holiday we took scooter rides home from the bar one night. My driver, a boy who looked about 16, spent the whole way home trying to kiss me, but his hair was so long he kept whipping me in the face with it rather than paying attention to the road. Meanwhile, Jemma's driver was confessing his love for her and refused to start the motorbike until she said she would be his girlfriend, which was never going to happen. Jemma was taken, and wasn't looking to start something long distance with a minor. Then we have Elissa aka Trudy. She got home no issues and was already on the McDonald's delivery order by the time we got home. We learnt a few lessons that trip. One was, don't invite your drivers in for a drink as they might think you are now dating – somehow being polite went to going steady real fast! Also whatever you do, don't drink the water in Bali or you will be stripped down, hosed off and lying nude on the tiles in the hotel room trying to cool down from the worst case of Bali belly you have ever had in your life.

UNCLE JIMMY

We all have that one family member, the one that differs from the rest of the tribe. My Uncle Jimmy was that man. Do not get me wrong, I love the bloke to bits. He never had children, but funnily enough, apart from my dad's sister Jill, nor did any of my other uncles and aunties. Uncle Jimmy in the early days liked to refer to himself as Uncle Adventure. He would come from Sydney to our farm and go on adventures exploring with us kids. Obviously, he would wear a Fedora and carry a hiking stick, and we would set off to explore the farm.

See, Uncle Jimmy went through phases. He was either very high or very low. In later years we learnt he had bipolar.

Even to this day, he goes through phases. One back then was a fitness phase. As kids we had to sit on his back so he could do push-ups and show us how strong he was. Another was when he'd grow his moustache long and curly resembling a character from *The Three Musketeers*. He's been married twice and both times, from what we gathered, didn't end the best. The bloke had a lot of love to give, he loved smothering us, and through the highs and lows, we just got used to him being that way.

He lived with his parents for many years. When we went to Sydney to visit our grandparents, he would be living there. Uncle Jimmy is a highly intelligent man who loves cars more than anything. His room resembled a kid's bedroom, even at the age of 60. He had posters of cars and toy models of cars as well as a room full of books on science.

When we used to go over, it was like another episode of a comedy sketch show. Deda would always be yelling at Jimmy for something, yet the two of them were almost like best friends. Jimmy would overeat too, you would always find him snacking on something. When Baba would cook crêpes, known as palachinke in Serbian, Uncle Jimmy would always overindulge. Baba would tell him off and say they were for her grandkids, not him. Even though she'd feed him before we visited, Uncle Jimmy would beg and we would end up, when Baba wasn't looking, giving him the food off our plates. We thought this was just normal and found it quite funny seeing as though Uncle Jimmy was a grown man.

Jimmy was a private eye as well as a substitute teacher. Interesting career choice, but it made sense. He loved air-conditioned cars and he could sit in them for hours with a few snacks to tide him over. With his love for Maths and Science he enjoyed being a teacher. He also loved the idea of being a sub as he could whip into a school or class for a few days and then leave again. It suited his lifestyle of not really committing and worked in with his other career quite nicely.

As well as his love for cars and food his other love was women. Bloke was woman crazy! He loved talking about women and all the dates he had been going on. He reminds me of a mixture of Jerry and George from *Seinfeld* as he nit-picks and breaks up with a woman for the smallest things, such as, 'She was perfect in every way, but had cankles. You know when the ankle has no shape?' For him, the 60-year-old who lived with his parents and in his bedroom had model cars, this was a deal-breaker and he would end it with them.

Even on a recent trip to Sydney we overheard Uncle Jimmy talking about how when he goes out he writes his name and phone number on pieces of paper and cuts them in little squares that fit perfectly in his top pocket, then he walks up to a woman and says, 'Call me sometime'. The vision is just too good. Call me old-fashioned, but I thought the man asked the woman for her number, not just wheeled and dealed his digits like he is working a business meeting.

God love the bloke, and points for trying!

UNCLE BRUCE

Bruce, Jimmy's brother, was the cool uncle when we were younger. He has a great sense of humour and I think in a way is very similar to Mum. He's the baby of the family and always the naughty one.

When we were kids he would come to the farm from Sydney, tell us jokes, teach us karate moves and spend the day with us. He was married to a lady who we grew up calling our aunty and they were together for quite some time. Unfortunately, that relationship ended nastily too, with her taking off and going MIA.

But he met a new bird, fell head over heels, so the story goes. When we first saw her, we thought, wow, she's cool. She was an artist and Canadian, she was blonde with lovely wavy hair, she was curvy and had a real presence about her.

The first time we met her was at their wedding. It was a small garden wedding at my grandparents' in Sydney, with just family, us, Baba and Deda and Uncle Jimmy. They look the part, all smiles and smitten. Romance was surely alive.

Things are not always what they seem, though, and this came crashing to a dramatic end.

We had Christmas and events at our house, and they would come and visit and we would all think what a cool couple they made. They seemed happy but as the day went on, so did the drinking. Turned out Ms Canada was a recovering alcoholic. The honeymoon period was ending real fast and the good times were being replaced by clear warning signs that there was trouble in paradise.

My Baba was an excellent judge of character and if she didn't like you, you would be well in the know. Baba smelled a rat and the cracks were beginning to form.

We have to fast forward a little bit to when my Baba got very sick, and when we lost her, she was the first family member to pass away. My heart broke when I got the call in Melbourne. Baba was a hard woman, she was a woman of so much glamour and class, she forever looked like a film star and she loved her grandkids endlessly.

We all knew Baba despised Ms Canada, including Ms Canada, but at the funeral, boy did she play the part of the grieving daughter-in-law. She wore a big black hat and from the outside looked like she was dabbing away tears for most of the service, when in fact she was sweaty and mopping her moist brow.

Mum had been living on the Central Coast, but when my Baba passed away, it was a good time for her to go back to her roots and move to Sydney. She moved in with her father and Jimmy.

The house was big, so there was enough room for everyone. Things seemed to be okay. Mum cooked for the boys and enjoyed some time with her mourning father.

One day Ms Canada and Bruce informed them they too were moving in. This decision didn't make sense. They were a newly married couple with a place of their own.

Jimmy had been living with his parents for most of his life except when he was married, Mum was looking out for her dad and was there to care for him. There was nothing keeping her tied to the Coast. Her marriage had ended and she wanted to be back with her family. She needed it at that time in her life.

Right away we were suss on the whole thing. Not only did Bruce and Ms Canada just move in, but they also brought their three big indoor cats with them.

When Mum moved, she'd taken Mickey and Rumble too who, after growing up on a farm, were adapting well to the Sydney lifestyle.

From day dot strange things started to happen.

Firstly the drinking continued, and when this happened a big shouting match would follow.

Ms Canada also thought it was appropriate to walk around in a silky night dress or her underwear, which my Deda, who was in his nineties, did not appreciate.

Then the drugs got involved. I can't say what type, I believe they were prescription, but for someone who didn't have an off switch and a very addictive personality, it pushed the limits, resulting in more arguments between them, and the police arriving.

Over this time frame, Mum told me the cops had come on 11 different occasions. I was furious and began to not only hate this woman but despise my uncle.

Who the fuck did they think they were? They had created this toxic environment to live in, not only for my darling mother, but my grandfather, who was a man of such class. It would be frowned upon if word got out within the Serbian community.

She was an embarrassment and unpredictable. One day, while Mum was watching her favourite show, which at the time was *Desperate Housewives*, Ms Canada thought it was her place to tell my mum in her own parents' house, the house she grew up in, 'Olga, you're pathetic. Why don't you get yourself a real man instead of watching trash like this?'

I could have slapped the bitch then and there. I would just get so fired up and discuss with Mum a plan of attack to sort this matter out once and for all.

Mum and I knew something was up. We had a hunch.

I was determined to find out what her problem was, and who she was, this mystery woman. Why was she in my grandparents' house? She was up to something and we needed answers fast.

We started to put together a bit of background info. Where had Bruce been hanging out when he met her?

Kings Cross.

He was recently single and was hitting the town hard.

Ms Canada worked nights, Bruce used to take her and pick her up.

At first, we were told she was a massage therapist, but I know they didn't work nights.

A bar maybe? A nightclub? Didn't make sense, she wasn't able to control herself around alcohol and drugs, so this environment wouldn't be right.

Did she drink because she was unhappy, or was it something more?

The other part we had worked out is, she had a bit of a sexual vibe. Not only had she been known to walk around in her underwear, she had also suggested giving my Deda a few massages.

Mum was the one who lived there, so I needed her to do more digging. She told me she had found a bag with saucy underwear and some toys in it, and I am not talking a bouncy ball here.

She must have been a call girl. I was convinced, but we needed some hard proof. For now, it was only speculation.

One day, Mum was emptying the bins. The only rubbish in the bin in the upstairs bathroom was two bits of paper, so instead of throwing the bag out, she bent down to pick them up.

She called me right away. On one piece it said 'STD test' and on the other, 'Josie'. Josie, hmmm. She loved cats. Was Josie and the Pussycats her code name for work? Was the STD test for her because of the work she did?

When I was next in Sydney, I got together with my girls to hash out where we were up to in the case of Ms Canada. I wondered, if one was working as a call girl, or something of that nature, where would one advertise. They told me to look at the local paper, they always had a page at the back listing adult services.

On my way home from our catch-up I grabbed as many papers as I could. Mum and I flicked to the adults' section. Bingo! Our hunch had turned into a bombshell. Sure enough, there it was:

> JOSIE
> curvy blonde Canadian
> long wavy hair
> mid-forties
> cheeky, fun and flirtatious

You are kidding me, it was her! We actually found her, and it was that easy. The ad had a link to a website and an address.

That afternoon we went to speak to Uncle Jimmy aka the private eye and my Deda to work out the next steps. Deda said we should leave it up to them, I had done enough research and he would now take action. I later found out by action he meant hiring a private eye (not my Uncle Jimmy) to investigate. There were photos and documents and statements; turns out I was on the money. She was an escort. Unbelievable! Did my Uncle Bruce know? Well, my Deda confronted him and told him they had to leave otherwise if this got out the family name would be ruined.

There was a lot of pride involved in this situation. I still don't know to this day what my uncle was thinking, or if he knew. Was he trying to save her? Either way, that marriage ended, and we never spoke of it again.

It took many years for me to speak to my uncle again. It really broke my mum's heart when her little brother decided to treat his family like that, allowing all the arguments and snide comments. They made my mum feel so uncomfortable in the house she grew up in, and she'd had to put up with the disrespectful behaviour of his wife. It was disappointing. Mum had always idolised him and they had a special bond.

Thank goodness, years later, they did make amends. He was there for Mum when she needed him and he was there for us, too.

It's disappointing to know time and time again not only in my mother's life but in my life, men do fucking stupid things for the power of the pussy, so to speak.

They act insane and really, when it comes down to it, I can guarantee, because it's not a wholesome relationship to begin with but is built on lies and deceit, it is destined for failure, every goddamn time. I am someone that if you cross me, you can go to hell, and mark my words I will cut you from my life with zero remorse, but in some cases I do need to grin and bear it if it's for the sake of someone I care dearly about. In this situation, I love my uncle and we have made our peace.

COFFEE AND CHATS

Once, we found Mum's résumé and under hobbies she had written 'coffee and chats'.

This would have to be the cutest thing I've seen a grown-up do.

Coffee and chats were a normal part of our childhood, and as we got older it just became part of our routine when we got together.

Mum loved making black coffee, Serbian style, which is cooked on the stove in a special coffee pot on a medium heat. She taught us if you want the crème on top, you need to use room temperature water and bring it to the boil, and if you were feeling saucy, you could add a spoonful of sugar for that extra sweetness. You drink it in short black coffee cups, with saucers, and once you are done, you flip the cup over on the saucer, form the sign of the cross over it, and then sit and chat. The number of times Mum did this over the years is countless; even if I said I didn't want a coffee, there was a baby one with my name on it.

Mum loved doing coffee readings, it was her thing. She learnt it when she went over to Yugoslavia in her late teens. All her friends as well as mine loved getting a reading from Mum. She would get all into it and put her glasses on and use a pen as a pointer. When you flip the cup the coffee grounds leave marks that can form pictures. Mum would let you know the meaning of the pictures. She knew some just off the top of her head from years of experience. For others she would need to get her coffee oracle book, in which you looked up what you thought you saw a picture of. For example, you might see the outline or detail of a penguin, so you would flip to P and find it:

> Penguin.
> Key messages: unexpected competence, lighter approach.
> The Oracle says: whilst the funny little penguin

looks awkward as he waddles comically across the ice, he is the polar opposite in his true home, the water. Streamlined and athletic, he cuts through the water at lightning speed catching his prey. Watch out for a similar talent in another person or even yourself. Do not judge a book by its cover!

Mum would interpret this meaning to the person she was talking to. She had a good instinct and a good sense of guidance as she did these readings. It was such a pleasure for her.

It wasn't really the reading that we all enjoyed, it was the tradition she'd built up, and really, it was about the quality time we shared in these precious moments.

THE AFFAIR

I'm going to take you back to the farm by a few years. Just to get you up to speed, my dad had been working in Sydney during the week, so he stayed Monday to Friday down there and came home on weekends. He was working for his so-called mate Alan. We hated the guy; Alan was nothing but bad news. If my dad made a stupid decision, we always had Alan to thank for being the terrible influence in his life. But Dad was a big boy and had to be aware of his own actions.

This time was the straw that broke the camel's back.

Here's Dad 'working' for Alan doing jobs at his factory, running some deliveries around town. Then there was this woman named The Doc. Well, that's what Dad called her, Irina was her name. Apparently, she was a naturopath of some sort. From day one, even though I'd never met her, I knew I didn't like her and never would. I had commented, she sounds like a strange woman if you ask me, anyone who spends that much time with a married man.

My brother had met her while he was working down in Sydney for Alan on one or two occasions. Dad had mentioned that she thought Michael was just wonderful, a great young man.

The weekend of my brother's 18th birthday, Dad comes home with a present from The Doc for Michael. It was a gold necklace, with a charm of his star sign on it. It was a special gift and my brother must always treasure it. Dad asks me if I want to look at it.

'No! Why the hell would she buy Michael a gift? She is strange, I am not into her at all.'

That week, Dana was visiting a friend in Sydney. She randomly gets a phone call from Dad. 'Hi D, I'm with The Doc, she really wants to meet you. She wants to do a reading on you.' Dana picked up some uncomfortable vibes but didn't go into too many details, something just felt a little off.

This time it's birthday number two, Dana's. Lucky Dana, this time it's her turn to get an exciting gift from The Doc. Dad tells her it's a special ring and will keep Dana warm when she wears it. I think, of course the fucking Doc has got another gift for another one of Dad's kids, is that not strange to anyone else? This time there is even a card. I read it and it makes me feel instantly sick. Something is not sitting right, there was an uncomfortable feeling in the air. See, I was hoping that maybe Michael's birthday present was a one-off. Boy, was I wrong. Dad asks me if I want to look at the ring. I get pissed off and walk away mumbling under my breath, 'No, I don't want to look at the stupid ring.'

It is a Friday night. I am 19 years old and instead of going out as usual, I decide to have a night in with my mate Dennis. While we are at the dinner table, Mum makes a remark about The Doc, as she had been making up these herbal tablets for Mum and Dana to help them sleep and to relieve stress. She was a naturopath after all, or so we were told.

Dad replies in a defensive tone, protecting The Doc.

Then Mum makes a cheeky comment about Dad being in love with her.

Dad replies, 'Yes, Olga! Yes I am!'

'Okay David, well let's call her and ask her then!' Mum exclaims.

Dad, still not backing down, gets his phone out to ring The Doc. Look, I know they're joking, but it's really starting to make my blood boil.

I grab the phone and tell Dad he is acting like an idiot, then ask him why he would even say something like that? It's not funny. I can tell he has had a few drinks, he's annoying the hell out of me. At this moment I realise I must get up and leave the table, the whole situation is making me furious and I need out.

Later that night I come upstairs to grab some more snacks for myself and Dennis. I was living in our granny flat at the time.

Dad is messaging someone on his phone, he does this awkward little jump when he hears me. As I walk inside, I notice he has hidden the phone, but I could see through the back door he was clearly texting. He also has his glasses on, which is a dead giveaway as he would only wear them if he was reading a book or something important, not for watching TV late on a Friday night.

'Dad,' I ask, 'who are you writing to?'

I notice a delay in his response.

'Larry,' he replies, then after a pause, he goes back to the message.

Then I hear him say out loud on purpose, 'I just wish he would call instead.'

That just confirmed it's definitely not Larry, and I had that strange feeling again.

I get back down to my room and message my brother; it was his first night out at the local club since turning 18.

I type:

> Hi Mike, how is it? Dad is acting real suss. I think you should have a little talk to him tomorrow. He is messaging someone, he said it's Larry, but I know it's not. Anyway, have fun! xx

An hour or so passes and I go upstairs again, this time for some more beers. Inside the house it's quiet, everyone has gone to bed and there isn't a sound.

I notice Dad's phone on the fridge, that's the spot he always kept it. I think to myself, ah why not, and grab it. Dana walks into the kitchen at that exact moment. I tell her Dad is up to something and I'm checking his phone. I scroll through the Nokia and notice the inbox is empty, all the messages are gone. Deleted?

Why would Dad delete messages from his inbox and especially, why would he delete a message from Larry?

Dana casually suggests checking the sent items. Genius! Why didn't I think of that?

Straight up I see at least 12 messages there, all to The Doc! I expected to see a little hint, you know, something to give him away. My father has never written me a text message in his life.

I was numb, I didn't expect to see the evidence I had been suspecting.

The first sent message read:

I LOVE YOU.

The second one:

I LOVE YOU.

Another message:

BE STRONG, I LOVE YOU.
TONIGHT, I TOLD OLGA THAT I LOVE YOU.

WHAT THE ACTUAL FUCK!!! It hit me like a tonne of bricks.
MY DAD WAS HAVING AN AFFAIR!!

I was slapping myself; I honestly didn't know what to do. Dana looks puzzled, confused and in quite some shock. We run into Dana's room and slam the door. We are sitting on her bed and I realise I'm still holding the phone. Instincts take over. I go straight to the contacts, find The Doc and hit call.

It's ringing and I am crying and shaking at the same time.

There is a pause then an answer.

'Hi,' I say, 'this is Tania, David's daughter. The one you haven't met yet or bought gifts for.'

I try to slow my breathing but I know my voice comes out more raspy and deeper the more I am trying to stay calm.

There is a pause on the line.

So I keep going.

'I have just been wondering if you have been texting my father tonight?'

There is another pause.

'Um, ah…'

She says something in Russian. Well, I think it's Russian as I have heard Dad gloating that she's Russian.

My heart is beating so fast, I am holding my hand to my chest to keep it from jumping out of my body.

I ask again, louder this time, more forceful.

'Have you been texting my dad tonight? And tell me the fucking truth as I have seen the sent items!' I demand.

The phone goes dead. The bitch hung up on me! My blood is actually boiling, I can feel it, and hear my heart beat louder and louder.

I hit recall, there is no answer!

I ring again. It rings out! I ring again and the phone is now switched off.

'That fucking slut!' I yell. 'I knew it! I fucking knew it!'

I know I have gone crazed; I can feel the anger rising.

I call my brother next. It's loud when he answers. He's still at the club and I can tell he's been drinking.

I yell into the phone, 'Dad is having an affair!' He cries out, 'I am going out the front, come get me now!'

I walk back down to my room. Dennis is confused. I've been gone a lot longer than planned and I don't have the extra six-pack of beers as promised.

As soon as I walk into the room, I burst into tears. He is hugging me and doesn't know what to do as he doesn't know what has just happened. I am now sitting on my bed, trying to get the words out, but I am sobbing, really sobbing. Years later when we reflect on this moment, he tells me he will never get over seeing me the moment my heart broke, he will never forget the heartbreak in my face. I try to explain, tell him I have just found out my dad is having an affair.

Next thing I know, we are driving to the Beachie to pick our brother up. There are so many thoughts racing through my mind, Dennis is holding my hand and before I realise it, we are already there. We can see Michael and his mates running down the street, I can tell my brother is drunk and confused. I don't know what to say so I pass him the phone. We drop Dennis off somewhere, and as we are driving home to the farm, we try to come up with a plan.

My brother calls Alan, the man Dad has been working for in Sydney, and starts asking him all these probing questions, to get as much information as we can. We want to know where Dad has been staying in Sydney. Alan explains that Dad stays with him most of the time. *Most* of the fucking time? He is there five days a week, we don't have money as a family to waste on extra accommodation, especially for her! My blood is still racing, and my heart is pumping. Is this what having a heart attack feels like?

When we get home, we all go down to my room. I crack a beer, the others follow suit. We are upset, angry. I just couldn't get my vision to focus, so many salty tears were in my eyes. It's now 1am and I can't sleep, I am wired. We finally all agree the best plan is to wait till morning. It's now 2am. Michael has just fallen asleep. Dana and I seem to be getting more crazed by the hour. I remember thinking, I don't even think I could sleep if I was drugged, I had too much going through my mind, too many theories, I was playing through all these scenarios. I couldn't switch off.

I had had a strange feeling for a long time. The night seemed just so long; this was torture. As I lay there with my eyes wild and wide, I was thinking, how? When? Why?

I hated him so much! How could he do this to our beautiful mother, to think my dad was having an affair was so surreal. What happens if I tell Mum and she gets in a car crash? Or I confront Dad and he gets in the car and ends up driving off a cliff? What happens next? Are we still a family? Who is this Russian whore? It was now 3.30am and I felt even more insane.

I remember Dana getting up to go to the bathroom, it was early morning. We hear the back door open; we still didn't have a plan. What if Dad came into my room looking for his phone? What would we do then? I had spent the whole night thinking and I didn't have a clue where to start.

We then hear the door close again and we know he has gone inside. We wake Michael up, we need to come up with a plan, a clear game plan. But I couldn't fucking think straight because all I could see were the words I LOVE YOU. I LOVE YOU.

The thought of those messages actually made me want to be sick. It was all just too much.

It's 6.30am now and Dad comes back outside, we hear him dialling a number on the home phone and realise he is calling his own phone. We try to mute the sound with a pillow, we haven't slept a wink and it's all just feeling like a dream, or more like a nightmare. I was done. I needed to get out of that room, we needed to do something. I couldn't handle another moment of this torment.

First, I march out of the bedroom. Dad sees me and smiles and says, 'Morning, Tunny.'

I just walk by and completely ignore him, don't even glance his way. Dana walks out next and follows in my footsteps, also ignoring Dad. Lastly is Michael. Dad walks straight up to him and asks if he has his phone. 'Yes. It rang and woke me up, so I put it on silent.'

Dad knew something was up, that strange feeling was in the air, an electric feeling of high voltage.

I march into Mum and Dad's room. Mum looks up at me. This early, she's still lying in bed. She looks so innocent, in her cute PJs, all snuggled up.

'Morning, Sweetie.'

I didn't know how to reply, I didn't know what to say. Mum must have sensed something was wrong and asked me. All I could do was nod my head.

'Okay, let me just go to the bathroom and wash my face, then we can talk.'

I managed an 'okay'.

I went straight to my brother's room. He told me, 'You do the talking, I will be the back-up.'

Dana was standing by the door when Dad walked up and gave her an affectionate hug.

'Don't fucking touch me!'

Everything then just happened so fast, it was a blur.

All I recall is pointing my finger at my father while sitting on Michael's bed and shrieking, 'YOU ARE HAVING AN AFFAIR, DON'T YOU DARE LIE TO ME!' I spat the words at him.

All Dad could do was nod his head. 'Yes,' he mumbled. 'Yes!'

How could this be real life? Suspicion is one thing, but I didn't know he would just blankly agree like that, no real emotion except sadness seeping through his eyes.

I was prepared to prove my case! My body was not ready for an answer, just like that, and from lack of sleep I was extra twitchy and sensitive.

I started screaming questions at him, I was yelling everything, all I could feel was disgust.

Mum then lightly touched my arm and said, 'It's all right, Sweetie, it's okay. I knew something like this was going to happen. Your father and I had been drifting apart.' She was trying to see reason.

It didn't help though, I was too mad, too angry, too hurt! Now I was shaking.

'You have gone and fucked it all up, you have fucked everything, you coward! How dare you sleep in our house, in the same bed as Mum?' I couldn't stop, I was on a roll now.

'You live in Sydney with her during the week, then on weekends you drink yourself to sleep, you are pathetic! You don't even leave us enough money to survive. You disgust me!' The words wouldn't stop pouring out.

'How long has this been going on for, David?' Mum asks.

'Six weeks,' Dad replies, just barely above a whimper.

'Who is she, David?'

She knew who it was but wanted to hear the words from the coward's mouth.

'Who do we all think it is? It's her, The Doc!' I exclaim.

'Have you slept with her?' Mum cries, sounding like a little girl.

Nobody says a thing, there is just silence.

'I can't do this right now, I have to get ready for work,' and with that, Mum leaves the room.

I had to get out of that room.

Michael was just sitting on his bed. He was in shock; we all were, but then he started crying. Dad tried to hug him and then Mum walked back into the room to embrace her son.

'It breaks my heart to see my son cry,' she hisses at Dad.

It was all too much. I was on the couch in the other room, I felt dizzy and faint.

Dad walked up to me, got down on his knees and wept in his hands. For a moment, I felt sorry for him because he was my father and I loved him. It was so hard to comprehend what was happening. I had never seen my own father cry in his life. I started to give him a hug and he put his arms around me. It felt strange. I didn't know how to hug my father while he was sobbing. He was trying to explain to me that there was more to the story. That he was in love, real love. That there was another man that wanted her, a rich French man. He had offered Dad $2 million to stay away from The Doc and never see her again.

Is my father fucking kidding? This is not real life, this is a scene from a fucking movie, it is not real life.

'It always comes back to fucking money with you.'

I was trying to reason with the bloke. It was a mid-life crisis, it was lust, he was infatuated with her because she was different to Mum, the feelings he had were all new.

He told me it was love, he was in love with her.

I felt instantly sick again, I was crying and then stopping and then whimpering.

Dad said, 'Just let it all out Tania, cry Tania, just cry, or just stop because I can't stand to see you hurt like this.'

Dad asked, 'Will you ever forgive me?' and then added 'because if it works out, I will find out on Tuesday and if it doesn't, I hope I can come back to the family and we can work it out.'

I just got up and walked away.

I went into my parents' room. Dana and Michael were in the bed watching Mum get ready for work. We all knew it had not hit her yet and were getting worried.

Dad walks in and asks Mum, 'Do you want a coffee, Olga?'

'Just boil the jug.'

Then he walks back in. 'Olga, do you want some toast?'

This was all too strange, he was trying to act normal. I was really starting to think he had a screw loose, that something wasn't right with the bloke in the head.

Mum kissed us kids goodbye and left for work. She told us she couldn't stay at home and that work would be good for her.

We stayed in bed, we didn't know what to do next. I told them what Dad had told me in the lounge room, something about there being a rich French man that had offered Dad $2 million to stay away from The Doc and she must choose between him and Dad. That in case she chooses the French man, Dad wanted to know if we would forgive him so we could go back to being a happy family.

'Fuck that for a joke,' I told my siblings. 'What the hell does he think we are, second prize?'

I would not be standing for that. He decided his family's fate the day he decided to sleep with a Russian slut.

I fell asleep in my parents' bed for about an hour with Dana, and woke to my dad asking whether we felt like a roast for dinner. For a split second, I thought the nightmare was over and life was normal again but then reality hit me hard. I got up and dressed, I had to get out of there. Dad was acting way too normal and it was doing my head in.

Later that day Mum called me from work. We decided to meet at Baba and Deda's house that night. Dana and I went together and when we arrived we saw Mum's car was already in the driveway, but so was Dad's.

We both ran in to greet our grandparents with a kiss hello. I went and stood next to Baba, holding her hand. Dana was sitting on Mum's lap. My poor Baba, her heart was broken, you could see it, her eyes looked glazed over like bits of glass, no emotion on her face, just silent tears.

Dad was such a fucking coward. Mum had to tell his parents for him. He was just sitting there calm and collected. I was thinking, what a fucking jerk.

My Deda just kept asking, 'Why? Why, Davey?'

I could feel my blood boiling again and yelled out, 'Because he was too busy thinking with his penis!'

The words just flew out of my mouth. I had never spoken like that in front of my grandparents before, but I couldn't hide my anger. Baba clapped her hands nodding in agreement.

The bit that got me so fired up was Dad actually had the nerve to announce to his parents that she too was Orthodox, the same religion as us. You want a fucking medal, you dickhead, I was thinking, not one person in this room cares.

Dana drove Mum home in her car and I followed close behind in my Gemini.

When we got home, Dana and I were on our phones calling uncles and aunties, anyone to get them on side. The news hit hard; it was as though there had been a death in the family.

When Dad got home, we were all sitting in the lounge room. I asked Dad what the slut said after I called her last night.

Dad answered, 'You don't want to know.'

'Oh, go on David, what else could she possibly say?' I asked.

'She was pregnant,' he said calmly.

He said it so calmly it was frightening.

'What the fuck, she was pregnant?' I screamed.

My father had completely lost the plot.

'She was pregnant, but she lost it, she had a miscarriage,' he whispered.

'Oh, what a fucking shame Dad, what a fucking shame. That's sad news, so she was going to keep it?' I cried sarcastically.

Earlier that evening, Mum had told my grandparents that she and Dad had too much of a past, that they would always be friends. But she retracted that statement the second Dad opened his stupid mouth. This story just kept getting worse.

'How old was the baby?' I asked.

'About six weeks.'

'Oh, so let's get this straight, the first time you slept with her you had unprotected sex. That's utter crap David, it couldn't have been six weeks,' said Mum.

My father was disgusting, I couldn't believe the noise coming out of his mouth.

I had to get the fuck out of there again. I went to a mate's house for a few hours, but I couldn't escape it. I got a call from Dana.

She explained there was more to the story. The Russian whore had told Dad she had the miscarriage on Saturday morning. She also told Dad he could thank his daughter for that. Because it was my fault I called her so late the Friday and I caused this. I'd had enough, now Dad was angry at me for killing his unborn spawn of a child from that Russian whore? I was so mad, who the fuck was she to accuse me like that? Maybe her stress came from fucking a married man that lived with his wife and kids, meanwhile she was also sleeping with a Frenchman that wanted to pay Dad off so he could have her all to himself. I was so fucking mad, and this was apparently my fault!? I thought I had felt enough anger and pain during that day, but this took me to new levels of rage.

I hated my father, he was the meaning of lies and deception. Once I got home, I couldn't speak to him. I told Mum he must get the fuck out of our house. He is not welcome back, after he stays the week with her, then wants to come here, no. He is done with us.

I know Mum had forgiven him time and time again, we all had. But it was too much this time, we were done.

I left a note saying he could find somewhere else to stay. The note also said:

YOU LEFT US DAD.

WE DID NOT LEAVE YOU.

NEVER FORGET THIS.

My brother wouldn't sign the note, it was still all so raw for him. He said it hadn't hit him and I understood.

Mum, Dana and I did, however. I thought it was a powerful way to get the message across that everything was not all right. We are not a happy family. This has left our hearts broken, our father walking away claiming it was for a woman he loved.

Mum told me that when he read the note we left him he started to cry.

'David, what did you expect? You have broken her heart.'

AVOs AND MEET AND GREETS

My dad had left behind his family for the Russian. We ended up moving out of the farm. We didn't let Dad know where we had moved to. He didn't deserve to know, and we needed a fresh start without him.

We ended up finding a beautiful house not too far away. To leave our childhood home was devastating. Our whole lives had been lived there, we had all those memories and we just had to pack up and go and not look back. But now we didn't want to be there.

I had never met the Russian, I had never wanted to, but now I was desperate to see who this woman was that had become known in our family as the homewrecker.

Once we moved out, Dad decided it was a good idea for the Russian to move into our family home. We didn't know at the time he was planning this, but I had eyes everywhere. One day as Dana was driving home, she noticed The Doc's car in our old driveway. A red convertible sports car.

When Dana came home and told us, I was so surprised, I nearly jumped out of my skin!

'What the fuck do you mean, her car is in the driveway?'

'I just drove past and saw it.'

'Oh, I am fucking going there right now. Who the fuck does he think he is taking her to our house?' I cried, anger pumping through me.

'What are you going to do?' Dana asked, concerned.

'I don't know yet, but I need a plan and I think the best thing is to say I am picking something up.' I'm confused.

'But the house is empty. We moved everything.'

'Not everything,' I say, grabbing a screwdriver, 'the shelves are still up on your bedroom wall, I am going there right now and getting them.'

'Oh fuck, well I guess I am coming too as back-up,' Michael chimed in. 'We can't let you go by yourself when you're this mad.'

We all piled into my Gemini and drove down to the farm.

I parked the car, my heart was racing. I was so pissed off, from the moment Dana told me her car was there, to the moment we drove in and I saw it with my own eyes.

We rushed inside through the garage, into the kitchen, me leading the way with Dana and Michael following close behind.

Dad was shocked to see me.

'Tunny, what are you doing here?'

I glared at Dad, and my ice-cold glaze shot past him directly to her. She was standing behind Dad, blonde, petite, younger by maybe 10 years. She had a harsh face and small features. Her eyes were dark and soulless. She was wearing dark denim bootcut jeans and a tight hot-pink T-shirt. She looked genuinely frightened as she hid behind my dad.

I held up my screwdriver, glaring at them both. 'I am here to get the shelves down off Dana's bedroom wall,' I barked.

Who the fuck was he to ask me what I am doing in my own family home?

In a calmer gentler voice, he asked me if he could introduce me to Irina.

I just stared at him.

'Why the fuck would I want to meet her?' I could feel the heat rising to my cheeks.

'This is our home and you brought her here.' At this stage she didn't even deserve to have a name. 'Why the fuck would I want to waste my time with her? She's a homewrecker and just as pathetic as you. What losers you both are!'

'Don't you speak to her like that in my house,' Dad roared.

'Your fucking house!? Your fucking house? Are you kidding me? This house was given to you by your father, it was our family home and you brought her here! You two are ridiculous and have no morals. Sleeping in Mum's bed, do you both even have standards?' I spat.

'That's enough, Tania,' Dad yelled.

'Oh, get off your high horse, David! Like I am going to listen to you. She's a smoker and you hate smokers, you are such a joke. You weren't even paying the bills, we had to leave when we had nowhere else to go! This whole situation is so fucked,' I cried.

'Tania, I wanted to introduce you, but not if you're going to carry on like this,' Dad replied.

I walked past them and went to Dana's room, unscrewing the rack from the wall with so much force I felt like I was going to snap it in half.

Dana and Michael were behind me, the tension in the room was high, electric. Nobody knew what to say or do.

I got the rack and hurried out the back into the kitchen. Dad was standing there by himself with a look of defeat across his face.

'Tania, I really think you just need to…' Dad tried.

I interrupted. 'Don't fucking tell me what to do. Where is she?' I looked around. She'd gone to her car and was sitting in it with the doors locked.

'You are kidding me, what a fucking pussy. She can't even look me in the eyes, hiding in her car!'

I went out there. 'You going to make some more pills? More anti-stress pills to give my mum again while you have an affair with my dad? You are nothing more than a whore!' It felt good to look her in the eyes and tell her what I thought of her. 'We are out of here, I can't stand another minute with you two near me.'

I yelled one more time, 'I am fucking watching you, don't come near us or my mother or else!' I hurled the words at the car window making sure my message was received loud and clear.

We walked off back to my car and I didn't look back, the nerve of them, so disrespectful of our family home, Mum and Dad's bed.

That night once Mum was back from work, I gave her a full description of how the incident played out, from every word to every bit of body language. I wanted to paint a clear picture for Mum of what she looked like as I knew that's the detail she wanted.

Mum asked me if I could draw her. I tried, but damn my cute drawing style. The Russian homewrecker ended up looking like a bite-sized cartoon sweetheart.

Mum told me the picture was too sweet and she couldn't hate her. We had to laugh at my attempt otherwise there would have been nothing but tears.

After our meet and greet, the Russian began to fear me. Sure, it could have been because of all the words of hatred and anger I spat at her while holding a screwdriver, but let's be real, she deserved it. She made her bed and she could deal with the wrath of the 19-year-old daughter of the man she was having an affair with.

My Baba liked to say her son had a curse on him, a curse the Russian had put on him to make him do these crazy things all in the name of love. Dad called me up to let me know they were putting an AVO on me.

Well, firstly, I laughed because this had to be some type of sick joke, right? My own dad wanted to put a restraining order on me because I was not into his new girlfriend and I made that very clear to them and the world around me? I called up the local police station to inquire, could this be real? The young and understanding police officer explained that if I had threatened her or abused her verbally in person, over the phone or via text message, they could in fact put an AVO on me. I was still just a teenager, I didn't need a criminal record or a mark against my name. The police officer advised me to drop it and stop contacting her, not to do anymore pop-ins and just be on my best behaviour.

What was going on in my life, I was the one that could be in trouble? The whole situation felt more surreal by the moment. What the heck had happened over the last few months? What had happened to me and Dad?

I think the biggest feeling was the betrayal of it all.

Mum started divorce proceedings as fast as she could. Not before my dad begged her to take him back and for us to be a family again. Turns out the Russian must have thought my dad was a bit more cashed up. Affairs must be exciting because they are not real life, it's an escape from the one you have that you must be unhappy in. They lasted maybe two months and it all backfired terribly. Dad lost his family, lost his gold-digging girlfriend, brought shame to the family name. He had a real shit run, but he brought it all on himself. He only had himself to blame, no one forced him to do any of that.

Turns out my dad had the farm, that we all thought was paid off, refinanced up to its eyeballs, more than it was worth. He had refinanced so many times, there was no way he could pay it off, he didn't have a job. How could the banks even lend to someone like that, I always wonder. He had also loaned money to 'friends' or 'business associates'. People that, let's be real, were never going to give the money back.

When the paperwork came through, my mum got $25,000 after being married to my father for 25 years. He had lost it all, gambled it on hopes and dreams. Thinking about bad decisions and terrible life choices, this is one that is engraved on my mind. I decided that I would work hard for what I wanted in life. I had been let down by my father something fierce and I knew I had to strive for greater things and I had the potential to achieve them. Us kids knew we'd never get an inheritance from our parents. We'd come to terms with that long ago. We would work and provide for ourselves. We didn't have a fall-back plan or a safety net, and we learnt that younger than most. My dad ended up living with his parents, he had nowhere else to go. Mum had us. Forever she would have us. Mum would give us the shirt off her back. She did anything for her family. With Mum, it was different.

BOYS, BOYS, BOYS

While writing about my life, I had a lot of notebooks and scrapbooks to turn to. I kept many of them over the years and the things I wrote about were always the same – family, friends, adventures, and boys. Looking back on these books in my thirties is entertaining, awkward and extremely cringeworthy.

I always liked to be friends with boys first. I guess that's how it happens in school. You get to know them a little bit, work out you like the same music, go to the same parties or are into the same subjects, or sometimes they are hot and you realise you want to hang out with them more, so you make their hobbies your hobbies real fast.

In high school, the first boy I had a proper crush on was Chase. He was tall (yes, even taller than me), had green eyes and dark hair, he was a great listener and was fun to be around. I remember going to one of those hippy shops at the local shopping centre where I got a wristband that represented love. When you put it on, you said the name of your crush. The story went, when the rope band snapped naturally, the boy you had a crush on would fall in love with you, or something silly along those lines. At 15, I thought, oh my god, this is it! He will love me, and we will live happily ever after. The band snapped one day at school, and Chase did ask me to the movies that weekend on an actual date. I was beside myself. This may well have been where my love for reading my star signs or going to clairvoyants came from. The reality was, we met at the movies because we both needed our parents to drop us off and pick us up. He got my ticket, we loaded up on snacks and I prayed my palms weren't too sweaty from nerves, but he held my hand the whole film. I knew this was what being a grown-up felt like.

Chase was the first guy in our year to get a licence, he drove a red Datsun and it was a beauty of a car. He would come visit me after school. At the time we had another German Shepherd, a big dog that was very protective of me. Chase used to bring out the Schmackos he kept in the glovebox so he could win the dog over, and with winning the dog over, he also won over Dad. Chase and I ended up becoming good mates. The love band wasn't right, there wasn't really a spark there. Plus, that first date I found out Chase was stoned, and for my first love, it would maybe be best if they weren't stoned for our first date. We made the right call keeping it as friends.

Another boy I actually dated in high school was too scared to hold my hand and kiss me, so that just made an awkward age and time in my life even more uncomfortable because as cute as he was, and geez he sure was, he was too nervous for a talkative girl like me.

Then there was Jackson. He was very cute, always smiling. We didn't have a lot in common, apart from hanging out with the same bunch of people, but he was the opposite of shy and a very good kisser. Jackson was a laugh to be around. This guy was really the first guy I would say I had adult feelings for and they stuck around for a number of years.

I wasn't ever keen on being in a relationship, though; I had commitment issues even at a young age. I liked the idea of dating someone in theory, but it seemed like a bit too much hard work. Firstly, you had to really get along, then you needed to have a sexual attraction, then you needed to motivate each other to do better, to strive for more, and the reality was, high school boys are immature and I was just as immature for anything to work.

Years later I met a man who I would've referred to at the time as my first love. Well, so I thought. I think I got swept up in a moment. It was the summer of 2007, that summer shaped me a lot as a young adult. I was discovering a lot about music; it was the first and only time I saw Daft Punk live, which still goes down as my top live music experience to date. I learnt a lot about myself and life in general, and met a lot of amazing people who are still in my life now. When I think about that summer, I always smile and think, geez we had some good times.

When I met Jack, it was new and exciting. He was not at all the type of guy I would usually go for. He was five years older. He'd been to university, he was intelligent, well, compared to the boys I had been hanging out with, and he was a real smart-arse, which I liked. I met him just before my 22nd birthday. We hit it off and I invited him to my party the following weekend. That night, we kissed. It was my birthday – I planned it that way. Kiss the boy you fancy. But afterwards, he told me he had a girlfriend and they worked as blackjack dealers on a cruise ship in the Caribbean. He was leaving in two weeks to go back on board for six months. You know my views on cheating, but somehow over the course of my young adult life, there would be a pattern that I wouldn't work out till I was older that without choosing to be, I ended up being the other woman. I didn't do anything to action this, but I tended to become a bit of a crush in the background. What can I say, I have good chat. I couldn't be painted with this brush, though; I despised 'the other woman'.

Jack and I spent that weekend and the next together with our mutual friends. Saying goodbye to someone you have a strong connection with, but who is also in a relationship is strange as hell. I felt like I had been broken up with, but I wasn't even dating the bloke. We spent a total of five days together over a few weekends with a lot of friends. I didn't have Facebook, and he left to get on the plane back to his girlfriend, his life and the Caribbean. At the time, I wanted to ask him to stay, but it wasn't my place. He was taken and I needed to respect that. I knew he had another life to get back to.

I had been acting strange. For a few days I felt like I was in a daze. Jack had left me with a note:

> There is something about you, girl. I am wondering if one day I will regret getting on this plane. I am so anxious I can't even have a cigarette, it was just our timing was off. Everything else was perfect I would say. I don't think I've ever had it that good with anyone before. Keep in touch gorgeous and don't think you're getting rid of me so easy   xx J

I couldn't stop thinking about him. Is this what being smitten with someone really felt like or was it just when you can't have something you want?

Mum, who'd been to see a clairvoyant, said the strangest thing to me when she got home. We were discussing the session as we were preparing dinner together.

'Tunny, Darling?'

'Yes?' I looked up from my chopping.

'Jackie said something quite unusual to me today. She said a boat was stopping and someone was getting off to see you. Does that mean anything to you?'

'Well Mum, yes, it does.'

Jack ended up telling me he and his girlfriend had broken up and he'd quit his job and was moving back home to Newcastle. He hated it, but wanted to give us a go. He thought what we had was real and he knew I felt it too.

'Mum, this would be a great time to let you know a few weeks ago I met a man, Jack. In three days' time he will be flying back to Australia and I think he is going to be my boyfriend!'

At 22, for the first time, I would finally commit to calling someone my boyfriend.

Jack really did hate Newcastle, it reminded him of all the reasons he left. He said he'd always wanted to move to Melbourne. I had only been there once, but had loved it. He suggested we move there, give it a go. The timing couldn't have been more perfect as I also had the opportunity to transfer there through work. It seemed the stars were aligning.

The feeling of packing up my room made me so sad. My whole life I had lived with Mum, I had never moved out of home before. My brother had moved away and Dana was still living at home, but this was huge, and I wasn't just moving out, I was moving to another state. I packed up my life into my Mitsubishi Mirage, and my dad, who I'd made slight amends with over the last six months, offered to help move us down. He was trying. Jack would drive down in my car, and I would go with Dad. I just needed to be close to family, it helped with the nerves.

I cried as I said goodbye to Mum, bawled like a baby. I felt instantly homesick as the thought of this possibly being a terrible decision was sinking in. Mum, just like when I was on school camp all those years ago, gave me the biggest cuddle and told me that if I didn't like it, I could always come home. Give it a go, she said, it's important for all young girls to live in a city at least once in their lives, and Melbourne, what a city it was.

Jack and I lived in a cute new townhouse, and even on a small wage, we made it as much a home as possible. Jack being older taught me a lot of things, opened me up to more music. He was an excellent DJ, had great taste in music, art and film, and he had travelled the world. I taught him a lot of things too. Looking back, I'd like to think I taught him to be a kinder person, but I don't know if this is true. I know he idolised me; he was in love with me.

He didn't really have a career and seemed to drift his way through jobs he was disinterested in. At the time, I was working in retail, and that's my passion, but he did it as he had nothing else going, and it showed. He was so negative about it.

We were extremely different. He was glass half empty and I am glass half full. This isn't always an issue; if you have the same dreams, hopes and morals, you find you balance each other. With us this wasn't the case, it got tired quickly and my motivation was getting drained. Sure, we had some bloody good times and made some memories, but to go back to that saying, that people are in your life for a reason, a season or a lifetime, I had to grow up and this was my reason. At the time, a five-year age difference seemed like a big difference in maturity, but what happens when you catch up? I was now five years older and Jack still acted like he was 27, like the day I met him.

He didn't seem to know what he wanted in life, or how to get there. He'd finally found a stable job just as cracks began to form in our relationship. He had to travel for work, and when I was out with friends or family, I never changed. I was who I was, I think that's why he fell in love with me in the first place. I was loud, confident, a strong personality. I could get attention when I wanted it and could make people like me if I wanted to win them over. The issue was, all the things he first fell in love with me for, he began to resent me for.

He started to get really jealous of not just boys – I had a lot of male friends – but girls, too. He got jealous of work or family, and before we had an argument, I could feel it coming in the pit of my stomach. He was also a tight-arse. He was earning a lot more than me, but we split all the bills like roommates. He had an addictive personality when it came to anything and he didn't have an off switch when it came to drinking.

It's funny when you are blinded by love. These things were always there, but just as my mother had said about Dad, you can't change someone. The more you try, the more conflict it will cause.

If women say something out loud, they have usually already been thinking about it, playing it over in their mind for at least six months. I do this often. I was playing scenarios over and over, but how the fuck do you walk away from a five-year relationship when you live in another state?

The straw that broke the camel's back was one night when I was meeting a friend for drinks in the city. It was mid-week, but I needed an excuse to get out of the house. He was running late to meet me and I was sitting in the bar by myself, which I had done enough times before. Two guys started talking to me, they had excellent chat and asked for my views on the discussion they'd been having, which was something ridiculous, but I was happy for the distraction. I ended up sitting with them for close to an hour. They were nice guys, one was tall and extremely good-looking, dark eyes, dark longer shaggy hair, very cheeky, the other was short and so sweet and funny. They were well-mannered guys and when you live in a city you aren't originally from, that's how you meet people. I've met a lot of people this way, by just talking to people in a bar. Not playing on your phone, I recommend it – it's very refreshing.

When my mate finally arrived, I said goodbye to the boys, but not before the tall one asked to add me on Facebook. I said sure.

That night I got home and jumped in the shower before bed. It would've been just after midnight. Jack came into the bathroom while I was in the shower yelling about something, I am not sure what about to this day. I just remember thinking what the fuck, I have just got home, I'd done nothing wrong, well, adding a boy on Facebook, but that was irrelevant at this point in time. I felt so attacked and it was clear he had been drinking alone. He slept on the couch that night and I cried myself to sleep. I realised it was over. I shouldn't have given my name to that tall boy, I got verbally attacked by my boyfriend and had no idea why, and all the thoughts that had been running through my head had come to light in the wee hours of the morning. As I lay awake, I realised what I had to do.

In the morning, I noticed an empty bottle of wine in the kitchen. When I asked Jack how much he'd had to drink, he answered none, but when I went to empty the bin, there were another two bottles in there. What the heck? He had drunk three bottles of wine alone, then yelled at me, and I was the one that felt guilty?

I looked him straight in the eyes and told him we were over. I told him I can't be treated like that and that he had a drinking problem if he had to hide empty bottles in the bin. I told him I loved him, but not in the same way anymore, and we were done. We cried and hugged and cried some more.

I think deep down we both knew it was coming. He packed up his things and went to stay with a friend. I couldn't be around him. I needed to think clearly, and seeing puppy-dog eyes and a tail between the legs, I couldn't bear it, I had seen it happen too many times with my mum and I knew it was over. Hell, I knew it was over six months ago, I just needed that final push to give me the courage I needed.

We gave it two weeks to clear our heads and work out what we wanted. I knew he thought we were going to get back together. He had reached out to me saying he would change, he wouldn't drink, he would get better, we could fix it.

On the drive to have the final chat after this break, I called Jemma. I needed advice, I was panicking. I had never broken up with someone before. Where would I live, what would we do with our stuff, how would he be, what if I saw him and took him back? I called her in a spin and she calmly talked me through it. I knew what I had to do and as she put it, I had to rip the band-aid off.

We broke up, I ended it. He thought things would go back to how they were, he told me he loved me and wanted a family with me, he wanted me to be his wife. This was news to me. The bloke was 32 now and needed to grow up and I was certainly not the one to do these things with him. I never really saw a future past the lifestyle we had and I had been over the relationship for some time, it just took me a little while to come to terms with that.

When we parted ways, he made my life extremely difficult and played the victim. He had burnt too many bridges and I was done. I held my own, but I was also nursing my own broken heart. See, I had the guts to do what a lot of people wouldn't have done. I broke up with him the right way in my opinion. I didn't cheat, I didn't lie, I was honest and I thought a part of him would have respected me for that. We couldn't fix it, but he resented me and I was starting to dislike everything about who he was and who I was around him.

We had a wedding in Newcastle not long after, which we were meant to go to together. We were put at tables at opposite ends of the venue. It had been a few months since the break-up. I had moved in with one of my best mates from high school who also lived in Melbourne. I hadn't seen Jack or spoken to him apart from a few nasty messages and phone calls he had left for me. I wanted to be a grown-up and loved the couple who were getting married dearly. They met the same summer Jack and I met.

Unfortunately, the wedding was a really tough time for me. While we were at the bar at the same time, I said hello. He told me to fuck off and not speak to him for the rest of the evening.

At this wedding we were all meant to DJ, we all had set times; I was on after Jack. But Jack wouldn't get off the decks, he refused. Every time I told him it was my turn, he would ignore me. The DJ decks and dance floor were in front of everyone, so all our mutual friends could see these altercations taking place. Finally, I went up again and he gave me not just one but too middle fingers, double fucking birds, and told me to fuck off. It was then when, god bless him, a friend told him to step away from the decks and it was my time to shine.

I don't think in my whole life I have tried as hard to hold back tears. How embarrassing, all our friends seeing this, weren't we grown-ups? How did it come to this? I knew I had made the right decision, but this just clarified everything. Bloke did need to grow up, he was acting like a child.

That night there was an afterparty, but I didn't want to be near my ex, didn't even want to be in the same suburb as him. I went out with a few lads that were keen to kick on with me at the club. I needed to let off some steam. I was drunk, mad and upset, and I felt pretty damn abandoned by the world.

So I did what any 26-year-old would do in my situation. I got more intoxicated, danced, did shots and went home with the hottest dude I could find. God, I wish this story had a better ending. I should have heard the alarm bells. He was a few years older, had long blonde surfer hair – we were in Newcastle after all – but he was a PE teacher, and you know, they are always the strange ones. He told me he was staying at his parents' house while they were overseas. Truth be told, I think the guy still lived with his parents. The next morning, not only did I wake to a throbbing headache caused by all the champagne, shots, beer and whatever else I had consumed at the bar, but old mate was obsessed with me. He wanted to take a photo of me to remember the night by – if you ever say that to a woman, she will think you are a stalker right away. It's called a one-night stand for a reason. Then he wouldn't call me a cab until I gave him my phone number. Being a genius, I gave him my number with the last few digits mixed up. I was not in the mood for this shit. I wanted to hit the showers and wash away my sorrows and scrub my soul clean.

Hindsight is a wonderful thing.

Jack was good for me when I needed to grow up, and I learnt a lot about myself as a woman and for that I do thank him. I moved to this wonderful city that I now call home, I wouldn't have met the amazing people who are now not just my friends, we are family, and I would never have met my husband if it hadn't been for moving to another state, out of my comfort zone.

I also learnt what I want in a man. I wanted a man who is going to provide for me, has strong family values, someone who respects me and never lies to me and will always love me for who I am and empower me to stand tall and be proud. And someone who isn't jealous, that is a big one. You have to trust each other, without trust it's impossible to commit. See, if I didn't learn these life lessons, I could have been dating a few more Mr Wrongs before I met Mr Right. It's a path I was meant to go on and I can't regret it, even if it hurt at the time.

Oh, and in case you were wondering about the PE teacher I gave the wrong number to, about two months later, I was sitting at home and my phone rang. It was an unknown number.

'Hello?'

'Hello, Tania?'

'Yes,' I nodded, slightly puzzled.

'Oh my god, I am so happy it's you, you won't believe it! Turns out you gave me the wrong number and I have tried so many combos and I just can't believe it is finally–'

The line goes dead. I've hung up.

Oh my god, it was him! How many numbers do you have to try when you give the wrong last three digits, I do not even want to know. I blocked that number and vowed never to speak of him again, until now of course. Like they say, you've got to kiss a few frogs before you meet your prince, and seeing this bloke had green carpet in his bedroom, I reckon I wasn't too far off.

MELBOURNE

Moving to Melbourne was one of the most life-changing things I have done. When I moved, apart from Jack, I knew no one. I had completely packed up and started a new life, far away from the Central Coast. Sure, it was overwhelming and frightening, but it was also empowering and exciting.

One of the first things I noticed was I had to learn how to make friends, not be friends because you grew up in the same area or went to the same school, but because you want to get to know that person, spend time with that person. I have so many amazing memories of meeting new people through work, bars or even at gigs.

A girl I had met in New South Wales a handful of times was living in Melbourne too. I nicknamed her Swiggy because we once strolled down the street while swigging from a bottle of wine – I know, how ladylike of us – but it's moments like these that you remember forever and they always bring a smile to my face. We ended up working at the same department store. We organised a night out, it was a new store and we thought it could be the first of many girls' nights out. Coolio, famous for 'Gangsters' Paradise' was playing a concert. It was the perfect occasion, so we rounded up a bunch of girls and got tickets. Plot twist, Coolio ended up getting busted bringing cocaine into the country. It was all over the news, and his show was cancelled. We still went out and had a wild night anyhow. It was the first of many and it was the start of some beautiful friendships. Two of those gorgeous girls, Briana and Lisa, are still a huge part of my life and were really the first friends I made in a new city all on my own.

Down the track, I also met Lucy, another important person in my life, when we worked together in my early days in Melbourne. I like to refer to Lucy as my sidekick, the yin to my yang, the Smalls to my Talls. She had also recently moved here, from Scotland, and it was love at first sight. The two of us have been pretty much inseparable ever since.

Along the way, I have met too many incredible humans to name, but you all know who you are and how important you are in my life.

Moving to a new city has its challenges and it sure can be lonely if you are used to being around family and people all the time. But it's rewarding, and just like Mum said, every girl should live in and experience the city at least once in her life. Amen, Mumma. Boy, was she right.

Over the years I changed jobs a handful of times and got to know more and more incredible people, and better yet, all these people I was meeting over time all got along. They loved my family, they loved my friends. My best friends from home loved my best friends from Melbourne. You guys know who you are!

Melbourne is a city with a life of its own. The food is sensational, you could happily eat your way around. The music scene, concerts and gigs at your fingertips – on the Coast I had to travel hours by train or car to see live music whereas the bars and nightlife here mean that you can easily go out for one beer and end up coming home after being at five venues, downing 13 beverages and getting a late-night kebab from Lambs On Chapel or a cheeky Wicked Wings box from KFC. Even at 5am you can still get a feed, it's brilliant.

Mark, one of my best mates from school who I'd been living with since breaking up with Jack, moved here a few years after me. He is such an amazing human; he is the life of every party. We used to have this rule, the roommates' agreement, which pretty much meant you had to do whatever the other person suggested if you added that line at the end. Pretzel! That's what he calls me.

'Pretzel, can we go out tonight just for a few sneaky drinks?'

'Nah Raisin, I am tired. We went out last night and it's been a big week.'

'Pretzel, come on man, just a few sneaky beers, roommates' agreement!' I agreed just like that.

It also worked in other ways.

'Let's go home, time to go home,' he would yell over the music at 3am.

'Nah mate, three more songs' or 'One more hour,' I would shout back with a grin.

'Roommates' agreement, three more songs and we go, okay?'

I would smile.

'Shit, all right! Three more songs,' he would cave in.

It was such a funny time in my life, we were always playing games. I would be watching something on TV in the lounge room, then my phone would start ringing in the bedroom. I would run in to grab it. The lights would be off, and as I'd run in to the dark room, 'ROOOAR!!!' A hand would grab my leg and I would have an absolute panic attack and then we would both die of laughter on the floor.

We also made excellent wingmen for each other. That's a lie – I made an excellent wingman for him. Bloke was terrible at returning the favour. He would always try chatting up a girl by making me chat them up. Most confident bloke in the world needs a wingman, go figure. The next day we would high five in the hallway after a night on the town if one of us had got lucky the night before. We were living our best bachelor/ette life. We would also have killer parties, invite everyone over, fill the bathtub up with booze. Lucy and I would raid Mark's wardrobe and come out in different hats and Jerseys, never a dull moment. On extra wild nights the house party would end up heading to a club, which more times than not, included strippers.

THE GERMAN

Speaking of parties, we had a killer party at our house for my 27th birthday. A bit of a backstory on two things. I had gone on a couple of dates with the boy I met at the bar the night before I broke up with my ex. It had been quite a bit of time since the break-up and I was single, so why the heck not. See, old mate was a bit of a Casanova, he had great charisma and chat, so I am sure he had no issues in the world dating women. But I was pretty new to the single world and not aware of all the new rules. I just figured if I liked him and we had been on a few dates, I could invite him to my party. Turns out this is Commitment 101 and a big no for Mr Casanova, but he didn't tell me he couldn't make it. It was more along the lines of sure, sounds good, if I have no plans, I'll try swing by. This did not happen. Old mate went missing in action and about three days later I got a text saying his phone died and he ended up at some party and sorry he missed my birthday. The writing was on the wall. This guy was going to be hard work and had bigger commitment issues than me.

The other backstory is that Mark had been telling me he was working with this 42-year-old English guy who was really good-looking and that he was inviting him to the party. So in walks this guy, and he is hot. Not just hot, model hot.

'Happy birthday! I heard you like Baileys,' he says as he hands me a bottle.

Look, it was news to me that I liked Baileys, but the bloke was so good-looking, who was I to argue?

'Thank you very much! You guys want a beer?'

The girls at the party all say to me, who the heck is that hot guy?

I nod, 'Oh, that's just an English workmate of Mark's. He's 42,' I tell not just one, but all the girls separately.

They all say in amazement, 'Wow, 42? Geez, he looks good for his age. He's hot!'

Here is me, still waiting for Mr Casanova to rock up, completely unaware of any other blokes around.

The night goes on and Lisa comes running up to me.

'Tania, he's German!'

'Who? Who's German?'

'The 42-year-old. His name is Johannes, he prefers Hannes. He is German, not English and he's not 42. He's not even 30 yet!' she laughs in my face.

We all head to the club close to midnight. The German, who's now been identified as Hannes, comes along too. Everyone is in fine form; I have almost forgotten about Mr Casanova ghosting me at my party. There were too many good people around me, oh, and the hot German, who I had now been paying much closer attention to. I had only spoken to him a few times during the party. He asked to take me to the bar and buy me a birthday drink. As we push our way through the busy crowd, I follow close behind as he leads the way.

We get to the bar.

'What would you like to drink, Birthday Girl?'

'A beer, a beer would be awesome.'

'Two Coronas,' Hannes tells the bartender.

'Oh, and a shot, two shots, two wet pussy shots!' I add.

'Also, two wet pussy shots, please.' He laughs then adds, 'Cheers!' We clink glasses and throw the shots back.

We head back to the dance floor. I take Hannes by the hand; he holds mine back. I don't know why I do but it feels good. I notice how busy it's gotten, there are bodies everywhere. I decide to lead him back to the dance floor the long way around. Halfway back, we stop and I make him sit with me for a moment on a bench seat. He goes to say something to me and I kiss him.

Again, I don't know why, but I do. It was my birthday and I wanted to kiss the hot guy that was so lovely, with the Baileys who wanted to buy me a birthday drink. He was foreign and sweet and it was my goddamn party and I would kiss who I wanted to, so I did.

By the time we get back to the others, everyone is laughing or smiling. Mark gives Hannes a cheeky high five. When I laugh with

Lucy over this story, she has another version of this part of the night that's a little different to mine. I thought I was smooth, cool and collected, but she describes it as me chasing Hannes around the dance floor before the bar and the kiss, and well, I love that version too.

That night Hannes came back to my place. We talked and I got to know his backstory a little better. He was over from Sydney, Dee Why where he lived. He was in Melbourne on a job, he worked in construction. Mark oversaw the job they were on. Mark invited him and some others to the party as they were from out of town. They didn't know anyone and he thought it would be nice. Hannes was only staying for another two weeks and then would be going back to Sydney. That night, a bunch of girlfriends were staying over. Mark was the ultimate wingman this time round. The girls were already asleep in my bed, so I couldn't kick them out. With his permission, Hannes and I stayed in Mark's bed.

The next morning, I woke up next to a smiling German. He told me it was a great night, and that even though he had a terrible headache, it was worth it.

I got up and had a shower to mentally prepare myself to start cleaning the trashed apartment. The floor was sticky with spilt beer and vodka and who knows what else. Hannes got dressed and as a well-mannered house guest started the dreaded clean-up with me. Halfway through his efforts, he sat on the beanbag in the lounge room calling out that his bad headache had turned into a bad hangover. I was laughing at him while I was doing the dishes in the kitchen.

'You can go now!' I laugh.

'What?' he says, confused in his now very noticeable accent.

'You can leave! You don't need to help me clean. I have this under control, it's totally sweet. Go home and enjoy your hangover,' I tease.

'I can't believe it! You used me!' he cries in joy.

He continues, 'You used me for sex, you used me!' He is laughing now.

'Stop being dramatic! I say you can cruise. Most of the clean-up is done now anyway,' I laugh again.

He smiles, 'All right, I can take a hint. I will go.'

He comes into the kitchen to give me one more kiss goodbye.

On his way out he adds, 'I can't believe it, I was used for sex! Woohoo!' Now his German accent was coming through loud and clear.

Before he leaves he runs back in and kisses me again.

He then adds, 'Oh, and you broke my belt.'

I feel my face go bright red. I turn around to see Mark laughing his head off.

I never gave Hannes my number, it was just a birthday fling. Sure, he was super cute, but after the last guy, I wasn't keen to get my hopes up, and I was sworn off relationships after the break-up. There was no way I could think of committing to anyone, but a fling was a different story.

Turns out Hannes had asked Mark for my number so he could text me on my birthday. Aw, what a sweetheart. The following weekend we hung out again, and the weekend after that was his last weekend in Melbourne. We spent it together. I helped him pack up his stuff and took him to the airport before his flight back to Sydney. Here I was for the second time in my life at an airport saying goodbye to a guy I barely knew, and it was a strange moment in time all over again. The difference this time was that I spent a lot of time in Sydney. I was up there every few months. Mum was living with my Deda in the next suburb from where Hannes was living. It felt somewhat more familiar this time, it felt comfortable already.

When I was in Sydney a few weeks later, we spent some time together again. Hannes picked me up from the airport and had booked a really nice hotel with a view over the harbour bridge. It was super romantic, no boy had ever done anything quite like that before. The next day he dropped me to my grandparents' house and picked me up again later. I had a party with my girlfriends and invited him to join me if he had no plans. He could stay at Elissa's house with me. That night he met all my Sydney girls, he had no issue meeting so many girls, he loved to socialise, and everyone seemed to love him instantly. I had been referring to him as The German and it really caught on. That night, we and another couple stayed out a bit later than Elissa. She was in bed fast asleep when we got back to her place. We tried to call her phone to wake her up, and knock on the doors and windows to get in, but it was no use. We were stranded. Me, The German, Jemma and Kenny were stuck on the street with nowhere to go. It's a funny memory, when you tell the hot new guy you are hanging out with, it's cool, you can crash at my mate's, but Sleeping Beauty just wouldn't answer her phone and we were stuck at about 4am on the street. Hannes thankfully remembered he had his car keys in his pocket, and seeing it wasn't the warmest of nights, cool for early October, all four of us piled into his little two-door car. Finally, Elissa woke up a few hours later and we headed into the warm apartment and slept.

That was the last weekend I saw Hannes. He had to drive to Canberra the next day as he was working on a job down there. I flew back to Melbourne and we said our goodbyes again.

Hannes called me a few nights later in a bit of a panic. His visa was running out and he had to either renew it through work or head home. He was also a bit flustered as his dad was building a new house and wanted his help back in Germany. The final thing that was making this all a bit overwhelming was just like me, Hannes had also recently come out of a five-year relationship and was not ready to commit to anything. I understood, but it got weird. He was still talking to his ex, unlike me, and she was also the very jealous type.

Again, I couldn't tell him to stay. It wasn't my place, I would look like a fool, I had just met the bloke. He asked me what he should do. I told him he was a big boy and could make up his own mind.

Hannes flew home to Germany. We didn't see each other again.

THE LOVER

Months passed, I had been seeing a boy I'd met at a gig. He was cool, had excellent taste in music and loved live sport. He texted me one night saying that I couldn't commit to him, that we were always just hanging out and I was forever telling him I didn't want a boyfriend. He said he wanted more. He told me he'd seen his ex at a wedding, and they had been chatting, that's why he had been quiet the last few weeks – he was trying to work this out.

He asked if we could catch up for coffee to talk about it. He told me I was a really cool chick and that he'd loved spending time with me, and asked if we could still be friends. I knew he and his ex had broken up because he'd had a chance to work overseas. We had talked about it and you could tell he was still fond of her. I said no to coffee and told him we were never friends so that too wasn't a good idea, but I did tell him he was an amazing guy and wished him nothing but the best. I thanked him for being honest with me – it was refreshing to hear the truth for a change.

Almost nine months later, I was lying on the bed one night looking through my emails and I found an old one from Hannes. It was a short and sweet email; he was picking me up from the airport and needed my flight details. Hannes left in such a hurry when he moved back to Germany, it ended so suddenly, I didn't even have a phone number for him. The number I did have was for Australia, and that was disconnected. (I'd tried it once before.)

I figured I had zero to lose, and he had been on my mind.

> Hey Hannes,
> It's Tania, how are you? How's Germany? Hope
> your dad's house is coming together nicely.
> What's news?
> Tania xx

Within minutes I got a reply.

> Hey Tania,
> It's so good to hear from you.
> House is finished, looks great. My dad is happy.
> I still have this and it belongs to you, you must
> have left it in my car.

Attached was a picture of my lip balm.

> How are you?
> Hannes

> Great news! Nice to hear your dad is happy.
> Oh wow, I can't believe you still have that! I was
> looking for it. It's okay, you can keep it!
> I actually still have your Oakley sunglasses case
> too.
> I am great thanks, started a new job this month
> and got a brand new car, my first ever new car,
> it's a Toyota Corolla. I am very happy.
> How is Germany, happy to be home?
> Tania xx

> Hey Tania,
> Great news about the new job and car! Awesome!
> I was also looking for that sunglasses case, haha.
> I think I may have made a terrible mistake, home
> is good but it's the same, nothing has changed.
> I miss Australia, I have been thinking of coming
> back.
> Hannes

> What, really?
> That's crazy, but super exciting if you do come
> back.
> Please let me know, would be awesome to catch

up if you were ever back in Melbourne.
It's pretty late now, so I've got to get to bed, new job and all.
Take care,
Nice emailing with you.
p.s. who actually emails these days!
Tania xx

A few weeks later I was going about my normal life. Over the weekend I was flying to Sydney to see the family, I had a christening, my goddaughter's. I was going to become a Kuma for the first time. I was super excited and looking forward to seeing everyone.

Wednesday night came around and I got an email notification. It was from The German. It read:

> Hi Tania,
> Hope you are having a good week.
> Just wanted to let you know, I booked flights and I am coming back to Australia. I will be there Friday, I leave tomorrow. I have really missed it and think I made the wrong decision coming back to Germany.
> If you are ever in Sydney let me know.
> Would be great to catch up.
> Hannes.

I was thinking, what the actual fuck, he's coming back, The German is coming back, and he was going to be in Sydney over the weekend, and so was I? My head was spinning, what were the odds?

I hit reply.

> Hey Hannes,
> Wow, that's such exciting news! I bet you're excited.
> Funny you should say that, I will be in Sydney on the weekend. I have a christening to go to, and I

am the godmother.

So I will be around, you will maybe be busy but I still have the same number.

If you want to catch up let me know.

Safe flight.

Seriously though, what were the odds! German was coming back, he missed Australia. This was huge, this was so huge. I had to get on the text line stat to my girls to debrief. Imagine Hannes, back in Oz. But I also didn't want to get ahead of myself, he was living in Sydney, I was in Melbourne. We weren't ready to settle down last time, I doubt anything had changed. I mean, I didn't want a boyfriend, did I? And he was from Germany. Calm down, I had to tell myself, chances are I won't even see him and he wouldn't text me, he is only just arriving that day.

I finished up the working week, my bags were packed and I was on my way to Sydney. I knew it was going to be a great weekend. I would see Mum, I would see my Kumovi, I was becoming a Kuma. I was excited. Friday night I got in late, so headed straight to Manly where Mum had moved into a studio apartment. Mum finally had a place to call her own again. Sure, it was tiny, but things had been looking up for Mum and the view she had there was just incredible. The best part was my Deda lived on the same street. He had finally decided with a lot of encouragement to move into a retirement home. He was 95 years old now, and it was the right decision. He still wore a three-piece suit for visitors and would comb his hair perfectly for any guest, even a nurse. It was a good time for him to have the extra care he needed. It was nice for Mum, and Deda too. As she was so close, they still saw each other daily, sometimes twice a day.

Saturday I spent the day with the family doing last-minute planning for the christening, time with Mum, my sister and my granddad, so it was a chilled day. I didn't really have plans that evening and the christening was the Sunday. Saturday afternoon I get a call. It's from an unknown number.

'Hello?'

'Tania?' A pause. 'Hi, it's Hannes.'

'Hannes, hey, how are you? Made it safe and sound!'

'Yes, flight was fine. I have done it so many times now.'

He continues, 'So tonight, do you have plans? I thought if you were free, we could do dinner. It would be nice to see you, if you aren't busy.'

'Yeah, that sounds good. I didn't have anything planned. Mum lives in Manly now, so I can just meet you there?'

'Yes, that sounds great. What's your Mum's address? I will come and meet you there and we can go together.'

He tells me he will be at Mum's at 7pm.

I tell him I am looking forward to it.

7pm rolls around, Hannes is on time – he is German and it's one of his traits I come to know.

He greets me with an awkward hug. We don't really know what to do, but both laugh because we know it's a little strange. It's been nine months and we pick up on the vibe that we both find the situation the same.

We stroll down to Manly chatting while we walk, conversation flows, just like it always had. Once we got past the initial do we hug or kiss greeting, the rest of the time it is really comfortable.

We spend the evening talking, laughing over dinner and a few beers. Hannes tells me that night he thinks he would never be the marrying type and would be a bachelor forever. I tell him he just hasn't met the right girl and if it's meant to be, he will know. I also tell him I am very lovable, so he has to be careful he doesn't fall in love with me. The extra schooner gave me the courage for a bold statement like that and I was being cheeky. I hadn't seen the guy in months. I had some catching up to do. Teasing him was kind of my thing. We spend the rest of the night talking about what the other has been doing over the last few months and tales of things we didn't know about each other growing up. The night is going so well that I almost forgot the time, well, until I get a text from my mum:

> Remember you are a godmother tomorrow. Kumas need their beauty sleep. I hope you are home soon. Love Mumma xx

Shit, it's almost midnight, the time has really flown.

It's time for us to say our goodbyes. Hannes tells me he will walk me home. He has parked his car on Mum's street anyway. Walking up the hill we are holding hands and stop to kiss. You know the strange thing was, it wasn't strange, it's just like last time, same energy in the air, and I know we both feel it too.

The conversation has slowed as we know the night is coming to an end and we don't know when we will see each other again. Hannes tells me he likes me, he always did, he wasn't ready last time to decide if he should stay or go, but this time, he knows he wants to stay.

He walks me to the door, we decide we will see each other again. We aren't sure when, but we know we both feel the same way and that it is just a matter of when we can plan it. He will come to Melbourne, he tells me he loves Melbourne. Hannes also wishes me good luck being a Kuma tomorrow.

From that moment on, as much as we didn't want a boyfriend or girlfriend, or know what we wanted, the one thing we both knew was that we wanted to be in each other's lives. We weren't sure how that would look yet, the logistics of it all, but in the meantime we knew this thing was too good to end.

Hannes and I started seeing each other every few weekends. He had moved to Queensland for work and I was flying up there to visit him or he was coming to Melbourne. He went from Hannes the German, to Hannes my German lover. We didn't really have rules on what we were doing, but it seemed to be working okay. If you asked me at the time, I would've replied, oh Hannes is just my lover, I see him every few weeks. It's nothing too serious, but no, we aren't seeing other people. Yeah, I like him but we don't want to be locked into anything. When really, everyone I spoke to would nod and smile and be thinking, ha, Tania doesn't even realise she's gone and got herself a boyfriend.

In February 2014, a few things changed. It was time for me to move out from living with Mark. His girlfriend at the time had moved in and as much as it worked okay, the three of us, I did not want to live with a couple. I found a super cute and affordable apartment in Richmond. It happened quite fast and I was very excited to tell Hannes my news.

He called me the same evening with some news of his own. He had been offered a transfer with work to Melbourne and had accepted the role. The next day, my workmate asked me what was going on as I seemed wired. I told her my whole life had just flipped around. Firstly, I'd got my own apartment, which was amazing, and secondly, my long-distance lover was moving to Melbourne. My mind was exploding, so much changed in just 24 hours.

I know what you're thinking, did Hannes move in with me? Well, the answer is no! I was not ready to go down that path again. I wasn't sure I would want to move in with a boyfriend ever again, I was still scarred from the last time.

He did however stay with me for two weeks until he found his own place. We decided this was for the best. I guess looking back it's silly to think we paid two rents, but you know, it was better that than moving in and realising the relationship didn't work. Remember, this bloke had never lived in the same state as me, and if you added up all the time we'd spent together, it was maybe three to four weeks, max.

A few thoughts went through my mind. What if I only liked him because I couldn't have him? Now he was here permanently would my feelings change? What if the honeymoon period was over, would he be wooing me with getaways at hotels and fancy dinners like he had? Do we actually really get along? Ah, there were so many thoughts. I just had to take a breath, put my grown-up pants on and calm the fuck down with my thoughts. Things had been good so far, we'd had to make an effort every time we saw each other in the past and we got along great, so why would things change? If anything, it was a good thing I'd get to see more of him.

In the time he stayed with me, we realised we had really missed each other, and it was nice not to have to wait a whole week or two to see each other.

Hannes had a wedding to go to while he was staying with me, it was on a Saturday, late afternoon. I asked him what he was wearing and he told me he had an outfit in his ute. A few hours before the wedding, I asked him whether he wanted to check the suit, make sure he didn't need to iron it. I didn't want to iron it, we had to have some ground rules for a non-boyfriend/lover that was staying with me temporarily. He grabbed it from the car, and looked to be in a bit of a panic when he came running in the door. You see, he'd driven his ute from Queensland, and somehow the heat from the sun had melted the sole of the shoe. The sole had come apart, not only on one but both shoes. They were flapping like his shoes had a mouth! He asked me if I had glue, but I did not. Next, he went to try on his pants and they didn't do up. I was laughing but he looked like he was about to have a panic attack. I asked him how long it had been since he wore this outfit and he replied over a year ago. Last, the shirt was so crumpled it looked like it would need more than an iron. By now I was laughing out loud at him.

He was panicking, and said the wedding was in less than two hours and he still had to get there. I told him it was funny for two reasons. One, I wasn't going with him. If he was my date, I would have killed the bloke for not trying on his outfit before now. Two, he was so flustered, which was just a funny sight to see, as Hannes was usually pretty relaxed and right now he was anything but.

He ran out of the house to go find something to wear. I was relaxing at home when I got a few picture messages from him to check if I thought he looked okay. The guy in the shop knew what he was doing. I said he looked very handsome, which he did! Hannes said he would buy it and be back shortly to change and go. I asked him what happened, and he said the guy working was quite flamboyant and the first thing he asked Hannes to do was to throw his shirt in the bin, but Hannes explained it was the only thing out of the outfit that fit him. The man laughed and told him that shirt belonged in the bin and they would start afresh. I adored this man and I wasn't even there. Look, Hannes is easy on the eyes, but his purple pinstripe Tarocash shirt and pointy laceless leather shoes were not his best look, that's for sure. The sales guy had excellent taste and dressed Hannes perfectly. Hannes came home with tan leather shoes, quirky loud socks, a matching tan belt, navy slacks, a blue striped tie and white Calvin Klein shirt. I asked how much his new look cost him – $800 later! I couldn't help but laugh harder. When I worked in retail, I used to love it when men came into the store in a whirlwind needing an outfit, and price didn't even matter because they had left it so last minute. I might just add, thank god Hannes' shoes came apart because no lover of mine would be wearing those pointers, but in this case I wasn't the nagging girlfriend yelling at her man, I was just the laughing lover thinking, I am so glad this happened as that will teach him for next time.

That night Hannes came home intoxicated. It seemed his outfit was a great success. He was telling me all about it while he ate the sausage rolls I had made over the kitchen sink in his socks, jocks and white shirt. He was trying to get out of his shirt but had got stuck as he'd forgotten he had on cufflinks, the only things he didn't buy brand new. He was stuck in a shirt he couldn't get over his head or wrangle his arms out of, and while he was in a haze of wedding romance, home-cooked food and beers on tap, he told me that he loved me and then proceeded to fall asleep still stuck in his shirt.

That's when I knew I had the bloke, hook, line and sinker.

THE C BOMB

Things had been going well in my life, Hannes and I were going well. His apartment wasn't too far away. The very first meal he cooked for me was a roasted turkey roll and a side of pasta. It was maybe the strangest combination of food anyone had put together for me and I told him, A for effort but next time some salads or veggies might work better. I did like the idea of having my own place to escape to, and let's be real, this might be the only time in my life I got to live in an apartment by myself, it's quite liberating.

One day in early March, Mum and I were chatting. I knew her so well I could pick up if there was a tone or something off about her. This time, it wasn't her voice as such, but she seemed distracted. After asking her again and again what was up, I finally got an answer.

'Look Tunny, it's not a big deal but they found a lump,' she said, in a tone that sent chills down my spine.

'Pardon? What do you mean, a lump?' I said in a voice that didn't sound like mine.

'A lump in my left breast, they found it in the scan.' Her voice sounds calm, too calm.

'Oh my god, Mum, what does that mean? Do you know what it is, is it breast cancer?' I cried.

'Yes,' she replied.

There is a pause. I am trying so hard not to cry. I feel choked up in the throat, and dizzy.

Mum continues, 'It looks like it could be, but it's small. It's so small. I'm having surgery. I am booked in for the ninth of April.'

Ninth of April, surgery, breast cancer, Mum, surgery, cancer – the words are repeating in my head.

I don't even realise I am gripping the phone so tight.

'I will be there, I will book flights.'

'You don't have to do that, Darling.'

93

'No Mum, I am telling you, I am booking flights tonight.'

I try to work out the date and the days in my mind, is it a few weeks away? We are only in March.

Mum is being strong; I know this is what she does for us, she does it all the time.

I ask if Dana and Michael know, she tells me she is about to call Michael.

'It's going to be okay, Mumma.' I tell her we can get through this like we get through anything.

'We will work through it and we will be there for you.' I am holding back tears so badly my eyes sting. I can hear my voice getting choked up. I tell Mum I love her and will call her in the morning.

That night I call my brother and sister. Even though we'd been living in different states for a while now, I have never felt so far away from my family as I did that night. My heart is hurting, my heart is actually hurting me in my chest. I feel light-headed and angry all at once.

Please god, please protect my mum, please keep an eye on her.

I am trying to calm down. Hannes arrives at my place, I'd been cooking dinner while I was talking to Mum. He walks in and he knows something is terribly wrong. I start crying and I can't stop, I try to get the words out but I can't. Hannes tells me we will work through it together; he is here for me and we are there for my mum. Tonight is the second time in my life a man has seen my heart break, again, actual heart break, but this time I don't have someone else to blame. As a distraction from the pain, I go to sleep thinking there is nothing I can do to fix things.

I go to work the next day, but something seems wrong. I feel hot, my breath is getting caught in my throat, my eyes, I am rubbing them and starting to see white dots. I rush down the stairs and go outside. I am trying to catch my breath, I am so overwhelmed in this moment and so scared. I can't explain how I feel. A lady I work with notices me outside, she can tell something is wrong. She tells me to sit and close my eyes and concentrate. She later informs me I was having a panic attack. The first and only one I have had in my life, it frightens me but not as much as the thought of losing my mum.

9 April 2014, I have spent the weekend in Sydney. I wanted to be organised so Mum was calm and ready for her operation. We have a lovely weekend, us girls and Mum, trying to take her mind off things. Mum was going in for a lumpectomy, the whole thing could take up to six hours. Mum was calm and comfortable as I held her hand, I told her I would be there when she came out and I loved her around the world and back again, like always. Mum told me the same back, it was our favourite line.

My mum's friend waited with me during the whole process. It did end up being a six-hour operation and although the surgeon had done it many times before, there could always be a complication. However, Mum's was a success. We greeted her on the other side while she was eating a sandwich and having a cup of tea, black, no sugar or milk, the way she always had it.

When Mum was allowed to leave hospital, I took her home and cared for her. I liked playing nurse. We had books, magazines, movies. I loved cooking, but dinner was her choice tonight. One of Mum's faves, being a Northern Beaches girl, was fish and chips. The hardest part wasn't even over. The following month, Mum started chemo and then after that would be radio. Her oncologist told her this would be the start of a long and involved relationship, but they would be there to support her every step of the way.

Mum started treatment just after Mother's Day. Hannes flew up to Sydney to spend that day with us and meet Mum, before she started treatment. I wanted Hannes to meet Mum as Mum, not as a cancer patient. To meet the glam, funny, dorky woman who had in recent years kept her hair short. Before she began chemo, we decided to get Mum's hair cut even shorter, just so it was less of a shock when it started to fall out, as we were warned by the doctors that was only a matter of time. Us kids decided we would buy Mum real diamond earrings this Mother's Day. We thought even as she went through treatment and had bad days and no hair, she would feel glamorous like she deserved, in real diamond studs, and she did! Mum loved them when we presented them to her. Not only did she love them, she also loved Hannes. It felt like a good Mother's Day and it was so nice to spoil her.

Chemo is exactly what people tell you it's like, it's fucked. Yes you lose your hair, yes your skin gets a yellow tint, yes your nails get brittle and weak, yes sunlight affects your skin and nails, yes you go off your food, yes you feel nauseous, yes it affects your bowels and yes it does make your skin dry and flaky, but if you get really lucky, it will help you kill off cancer cells.

Look, I know I have pointed out on a few occasions that Mum was my hero, but geez, the woman just handled life so courageously. When her hair started to fall out, she just shaved it all off and embraced her new look. Pre cancer, her hair had started thinning, and Mum was extremely self-conscious about it, but when faced with the news she would now lose it through chemo, she just went and shaved it all off like a boss.

Mum decided for the first time in her life she would wear a blonde wig. Why would she wear one the same dark colour as her hair? That's just boring. She added more colour to her wardrobe and insisted that it brightened her up. The months she went through treatment she never once complained. We organised meals and food where we could, and Mum gracefully took one day at a time. She was determined to beat breast cancer and wanted to hold her head up high as she did so. I just felt so proud of her, she wasn't a victim, she refused to even tell people she was going through chemo, and god forbid we use the C word. Oh, hell no! That was banned from day one.

DISAPPEARING ACT

Back in Melbourne, one night I had started cooking dinner after the gym. I was waiting for Hannes to come over. I was busy in the kitchen and listening to music when he called to let me know he was about to park the car, so I buzzed him in. It had been a pretty good day and Mum seemed to be getting through her treatment better than the week prior, so that was an awesome win.

Hannes and I had developed a routine when he came over. The first thing he would do is kiss me hello. I heard him say hi, and I started chatting away about my day, telling the latest tale I had in store for him. I noticed he hadn't said anything. I stopped and spun around to see him standing in the doorway. He had a beanie on which was strange as it was getting to the end of winter and the whole time I had known him, he had never worn a beanie. The weather had been quite pleasant that day for that time of year. I sensed something was up and asked him if he was all right.

'Not really, I've had an accident,' he tells me.

'Oh my god, are you okay? Shit, what happened?' I'm in a bit of a panic now.

He started to take his beanie off.

I look at him in such surprise, as what I am looking at takes me a moment to process.

Hannes looks like he is going to start bawling.

'What the fuck! Where are your eyebrows?' I yell in shock.

Hannes is standing there, with his normally thicker than average eyebrows, gone! Gone completely.

I then backtrack. 'Shit, sorry, was there an explosion at work today? A fire? What happened? Are you burnt anywhere else?'

He shakes his head.

He finally speaks, and I realise he hasn't said anything for such a long pause.

'I shaved it off by mistake.'

'I am sorry, what!?'

'I accidentally shaved one off,' he answers, more sheepishly this time.

'Hang on a second, I am so fucking confused.' I realise I've been holding the tongs this whole time.

'You shaved your eyebrow off? Just one, what happened to the other one?' I laugh.

He tells me he was trimming his beard before he came over to see me, you know, freshening up so he looked good. Last time he got his hair cut, he noticed how the barbers sometimes clip over the longer bits of hair on the eyebrows, the parts that stick out. Hannes was attempting to do that and as he did, the cover came off and took the whole eyebrow off. I am still so confused.

'You shaved your own eyebrow off?' Then I ask again, 'What happened to the other one?'

He tells me he panicked and didn't know what to do, so in the spur of the moment, caught in shock, he did the other one without thinking. I was trying not to laugh, but I was in so much shock.

'You shaved both your eyebrows off on purpose!'

Well, he shaved off one and then thought, rather than phone a friend or call his girlfriend, he'd just shave the other off to make them look the same, put a beanie on and hope she doesn't notice. Do you know how hard it is, when someone has eyebrows as a distinct feature and then suddenly they are gone, not to stare? Hannes looked like a completely different man. He looked ill.

'Hannes, you can't go shaving your eyebrows off. Is there something I am missing where all the people in my life suddenly have no eyebrows? You look like my mum, like a cancer patient.'

At the time Mum had lost her eyebrows; that, I could understand, but my boyfriend?

The poor bloke was in shock too, and I was not helping the situation. Hannes sulked for the rest of the night while I asked him, why both, why not wear a band-aid over one like Nelly or we draw the rest of it in with a pencil? Once I got over the initial shock, I felt bad and tried to cheer him up the rest of the evening.

We had a dinner the following week for a friend's birthday. I had warned a few of my close friends and even though we'd only been dating for a few months everyone really liked Hannes. When he got up to go to the bathroom, the whole table looked at me and finally someone said, 'Um, Tania, want to explain where Hannes' eyebrows have gone?' A few of them added, 'I can't stop staring at him, he looks so different.' When Hannes returned, no one said a thing. That night when we got home, Hannes informed me he felt a lot better and that no one seemed to notice, which was good and made him feel better. Little did he know!

Thinking back, this was the first fight we'd had – when my boyfriend accidentally shaved not one but both his eyebrows off and thought I wouldn't notice. It took them about six months to grow back to how they normally looked. When we tell this story, Hannes explains this is how he knew I loved him for him, not just for his looks. He says it was a test. Yeah right, mate.

SHACKING UP

After 12 months, Hannes and I decided it was time to move in together. My lease was up and his just a few weeks after mine. We were on the hunt for a two-bedroom place, and after dealing with a few crazy realtors we found the perfect one. This unit had just one other beneath it, and had off-road parking in a suburb south of Melbourne's CBD, close to markets, bars and all the action. It ticked all the boxes.

One of the first weekends after we had settled into our new place, Hannes and I got tickets through my work to see the Foo Fighters. They were excellent VIP tickets and the show was brilliant. Afterwards I invited my boss and his partner back to ours, plus a mate who had been at the show but not with us in the VIP section. Turtle and I were well overdue for a good session, it'd been too long between catch-ups. After the others left, we kicked on with beers and whiskies and music until the wee hours of the morning. Hannes went to bed around midnight, I tend to be the night owl in the relationship. Turtle was happy to keep going, as was I. We even turned the decks on. I have DJ decks at home. It was a little treat I got when I moved out by myself and I loved it as a hobby. Turtle and I were up drinking whisky and smoking cigars. I don't smoke cigarettes and as Turtle had run out of smokes, I suggested we smoke some cigars I had. We were puffing away having a real party for two. We started playing Joe Cocker, 'With a Little Help from my Friends'. An absolute tune, which Turtle loves, and then he started using an empty whisky bottle as a microphone because this is how he rolls when the song comes on, the man needs a mic. We had a cow-hide rug and I vaguely remember getting put on it and Turtle trying to slide me around the floor as if it was a magic carpet. Also, I think one of us was using a cactus plant as a mic at some stage. Not quite the safest of props, but at the time it seemed like a good idea. There was a knock on the door and being in the house for just over a week, I didn't know anyone in the neighbourhood, and no one really had our new address. I was greeted by two police officers telling me they'd had a noise complaint.

I apologised and explained I had just moved in, my boyfriend was sleeping and a friend and I were listening to music and having a few drinks, but I would make sure to keep it down.

The cop seemed shocked it was only two of us, and told us to keep it down and make sure there is no loud singing or music. We laughed and told him no problem and thanked the one doing the talking for being such a good sport about it all.

After the cops left, we knew we had to be better behaved. We turned the music down, and tried to tone our two-man dance party down a few notches. We had another cigar and one more nightcap for the road. We also decided it was time for one last song. 'Wonderwall' by Oasis surely was a great choice.

Turtle crashed out on the lounge, I went to sleep, and in the morning, woke up to Hannes saying, 'What the hell did you guys do last night?' The rug was wrapped over the couch and there were plants in the middle of the room, which smelled of beers and cigars. Hannes being a good sport let me sort it all out. He was happy to see our new house could survive a shindig with Turtle and me. I spent the morning cleaning up everything around the house. We had somehow managed to knock out the flyscreens on both windows in the lounge room, I think we needed more air floor when the dance floor was pumping. I went outside and cleaned around the neighbour's windows as well as collected the flyscreens that had fallen down there, with my tail between my legs hoping they didn't already hate me as I was positive they were the ones that called the cops. Surely, it had to be them.

After I cleaned myself up as well as the house, I popped over to a boutique bottle shop nearby. The man working there saw me browsing the red wines.

'Do you need a hand?'

I simply replied, 'What's a good "Sorry I'm a terrible neighbour" bottle of red?'

He asked me how much I wanted to spend.

I told him we just moved in and I think they called the cops on me.

He laughed and told me at least a $50 bottle.

I agreed it seemed fair and he picked one out for me.

I got home and wrote a note:

> Hi Unit 1,
> Sorry we haven't met yet, just had a few friends
> over for a housewarming last night and it got out
> of hand. Please accept this bottle of wine as an 'I
> am sorry' gift.
> Regards,
> Unit 2
> p.s. if you ever need to contact me just text or call

and I left my number. Almost a month later we bumped into them and exchanged a quick hello and introduction. Gav and Sylvia had a dog and seemed like a lovely couple.

I mentioned that for Easter I was cooking up a big Good Friday lunch if they had no plans and wanted to join us. They said they would love to and when they arrived they brought the I'm sorry wine. They explained it was such a nice gesture that it would be better if we drank it together.

This was the start of a beautiful friendship; these guys are still in our lives, just as present as ever.

I also had to come clean about the house party, and explain about Turtle and me getting super excited on the beers. They laughed and told us they weren't the ones that called the cops. They said we were loud but they assumed it was a housewarming. I confessed it was actually just Turtle and me they could hear. They said when they heard Oasis' 'Wonderwall', they knew the night was coming to an end so they didn't have to worry about noise anymore.

VEGAS

I love a good punt. Don't get me wrong, I don't have an addictive personality, but I'm not one to back down from a game of roulette when it's my last night in Vegas!

Let me set the scene. When I turned 30, I went on an epic holiday to the States. Thirty is a big one and it wasn't just me, it was my girl Fergie too, a double 30th in Vegas, or as we liked to refer to it, 'Fergie and Tizzy Tour the West Coast!' Plus, Fergie's brother Jay and his girlfriend Sammy were in town as they'd decided to get hitched Vegas style. The trip really ticked all the must-dos when in Vegas.

Our last day started like most days in Vegas, except this particular day was also Fergie's birthday. Bloody Marys by the pool, it was hot, we were in the desert; this day was a good day. It was our last adventure there. In the great words of Rick James, 'It's a celebration, bitches.'

By 7pm it was go-time! The plan was to meet in the lobby for a surprise – a limo had arrived for the birthday girl, champagne followed, then came a surprise helicopter tour of the strip at night, more champagne and before we knew it, the time had come to hit the club!

Walking into Hakkasan was like a scene from *Entourage*, as Jay described it! Sequins, posers, holidaymakers and all the wonderful interesting people-watching you would expect in Vegas.

Within minutes of getting a drink, we made our way through the ever so crowded dance floor. I was overwhelmed by how packed this joint was, no room for dancing unless you were a VIP, but no dramas, as by the time we'd made it through the crowd, we'd been hand-picked for some VIP booth action. Three gals and one guy… the girls were all good, but sorry, they say to Jay, girls only! His response? 'Oh, no problem, you see I have just travelled from Australia for my sister's 30th today! Not to mention I married my girlfriend yesterday, but please have fun with my wife and sister. I just want them to have a good night!' Within moments the man had embraced not only us, but Jay with his sweet honesty. He invited us all to drink with him and his friends, and enjoy the perks of being VIPs, which let me tell you, started with giant bottles of Grey Goose, fresh lime and soda.

We had found our happy place!

The party had really gotten into full swing. We had this talent of becoming best friends with everyone we met on our travels, planning future outings and events. This night was no different – making best friends left, right and centre.

It was almost time to move to the next adventure, which in this case was a round on the tables to try our luck with our new posse of Armenian doctors and dentists. Roulette was always the game of choice, and black baby, always black was my motto!

Didn't take me too long to work out our new friends were cramping my style and unlucky, so I blew them off to hit the tables solo.

Now, who knows what came over me with my newfound love of gambling. Maybe the combination of the free fireball whisky shots and Frangelico and fresh lime I was knocking back like water? Maybe that it was my last night in Vegas? Whatever the reason, I had become possessed! I did not want to stop playing! As I can still hear myself saying, I was on! I was feeling extra lucky and I also didn't want Vegas to end; this would turn out to be an interesting combination for one tall Australian lass.

I had learnt all the names of the card dealers around me and given them some pretty sweet nicknames too:

Joy (to the World)

Calvin (Alvin and the Chipmunks)

Daniel (the Boring Unlucky One)

I was playing with the big guns dropping $500 on black, tipping for drinks like I was Kanye West and to be honest, I *was* on!

Randoms were saying things like, 'I have no idea what this Australian gal is talking about as I can't understand her accent or a word she is saying, but she is having the time of her life!' Others were asking me to walk away as they couldn't take the stress of me winning and then losing almost all of it and then doing it all over again. Chips aren't real money, it's just a game, right?

I must say, it is amazing what free booze, loud music, VIP treatment and winning do to one's ego! The night was wrapping up and I was determined to win big or walk away down a few hundred. No biggie. Last night in Vegas and you only turn 30 once!

Before the night wrapped up I had befriended two Cuban men at the table, or as I liked to refer to it, the party table! These two men couldn't speak much English. All I know is, I had been referring to them as my 'Cuban lucky charms' and every time I did what they suggested I won. I was happy with that! Yes, they kept calling me their Cuban bride, and sure, typing that now, it is strange, but at the time, it made perfect sense as everything does in Vegas!

Finally the time had come to walk away and go back to the hotel to pack. By this point, it was around 8.30am and we had to check out at midday. I had left with nothing, but the whole night was free, so in my case I felt the hours of entertainment was money well spent! I said my farewells and stepped into the daylight on my adventure home.

It turns out my casino was a cab fare away, however when I searched for my purse, I realised it was gone. This was no good, never in my life had this happened to me. I was determined to retrace my steps and find it. I made my way back to the hotel, bumping into my Cuban lucky charms again while asking the dealer if they had seen my purse.

To my dismay, no luck! My epic high was ending, and swiftly. On the bright side I had nothing too valuable in there except my driver's licence and my dignity. Off to 'lost and found' I went, I left my details. The Cubans walked me to a cab and mentioned they were staying there, so if it turned up they would drop it at my hotel. I mean, sounded like a great idea at the time.

I called Fergie hoping she was there to let me in and pay for the cab. She assured me she'd be there when I got in. I was so happy to see her, it felt like it had been days. Fergie decided it would be a great idea if we swapped stories over a Bloody Mary at the table. By golly gosh, this was the best flipping news I had heard since I lost my purse! I borrowed the room key to grab my hidden winnings from the days before. (Yes, that's right, while it's much to my dismay, portraying myself as an addictive gambler, I had walked away with a quite impressive pile of crisp $100 notes during my stay so far and had hidden them from myself in the room safe. Foolproof plan!) I took a cheeky $100 note and back down I trotted to some more roulette.

We were both on this time, Fergie and I were winning! Then out of the blue, the Cubans show up. They just strolled right up to me. 'Can you come outside? It's about your purse, we need to talk.'

I was like, 'Fellas, can't you see I'm a little busy gambling, I don't have time for this, no I won't.' Cuban 1 asked me again, this time adding smugly, 'What is your wallet worth to you?' By now, we were all paying attention to the Cubans, even the dealer had focused his full attention. Cuban 1 again more directly asked me, 'Is it worth $200 for our trouble as we think we got it back, but there was a drama with security (blah blah blah) or even $100 to pay us (blah blah blah)...' At this point, my patience was really wearing thin.

I exclaimed, 'Are you seriously kidding me? You have obviously got my purse, I can see you're holding it, plus you would have seen a picture of me on my driver's licence. It is absolutely clear what has happened – you two have rolled me!'

I went on. 'You must have pick-pocketed me at the tables as I had no cash, nothing but chips! I'm not even mad, I'm just disappointed! What would your mothers think, I bet they wouldn't be proud of you, spending your morning robbing an Aussie girl who was just having a good time.'

With that, I snatched my purse back from his clutches.

At this point I also decided it would be a great idea, for more dramatic impact, to throw $60 worth of chips at him.

I explained that that'd cover my driver's licence and all it was worth to me.

The dealer had called over the security guard to get these two jerks kicked out.

They left with their tails between their legs, they had gotten the boot, thank god. What losers!

The dealer looked at me and Fergie.

'Are you okay?'

I said yes.

'Do you want to keep playing?'

I said yes.

'Do you need another drink?'

Fergie and I both exclaimed, 'YES!'

He also added, 'My favourite part is the way you threw the chips at him like it was nothing, not that I would have given him a thing. But it was great to watch him scramble to pick them up.'

And then I won $950! That is really how the story ends, I picked the right number three times, we left the tables, cashed in our winnings, packed our room in 20 minutes and left. Turns out time really does fly when you are having fun! Thank you, Vegas, you wonderful wacky and addictive place, I couldn't have had a more Vegas experience if I tried.

A PROPOSAL

The way my two best friends found out Hannes was going to propose to me was at my Baba Pera's funeral. Baba Pera was the last of our grandparents left. She was the world's most caring woman. She had a heart of gold, gave the best cuddles and always put her family first. Her warm loving nature just shone through her. The passing of a grandparent is always hard, and never gets easier even if they are 96 years old. They have always loved you endlessly and would do anything to make sure you were well fed and warm and loved.

At the end of a Serbian Orthodox funeral the immediate family stand in a line for everyone to come and pay their respects. A handshake and three kisses on the cheeks are standard, for closer crew it's a big cuddle and more tears. Hannes, who had been in the family for almost two years now, loved my family as his own. He was standing by my side, and my mum who was two over from me in the line started introducing Hannes to people as my fiancé. Here is me, mid teary hugs, looking over to explain to my mother, Hannes is my boyfriend not my fiancé. My two best friends overheard and pulled my mum aside afterwards to get all the goss.

Just six weeks before at Serbian Christmas, Hannes had asked my parents for their permission to marry me. He had also mentioned it to my brother and sister, which to me is respectful and lovely. I had no idea this was happening; we had discussed marriage and kids, but this was news to me. For Christmas he got us a trip to Tasmania, as neither of us had been. He booked a beautiful hotel, we had a few day trips planned, like Bruny Island, the Mona and a few more little surprises.

As you know by now, I am a pretty good detective, but I didn't see this one coming. I did ask at the airport why he had such a big bulge in his pocket. Which no, wasn't a ring, but was a tub of lip balm – he wanted to carry it to see if I would notice, which I did, and if so, he'd need a plan B, a backpack. But I'd asked why he needed a backpack for his sunglasses and lip balm when I had a bag he could use. He was acting a little strange, but no alarm bells had gone off.

One day, he'd planned a boat ride to get to a friend's birthday lunch. It was a perfect day for it, a bit cool for March, but the sun was out. On the boat, Hannes kept telling me he loved me, which wasn't really that unusual, but he was doing it an awful lot. I had to ask him to calm down, he was acting a little loopy; one or two 'I love you's a day is enough. Bloke had said it about 10 times just on the boat trip, it was wigging me out.

The venue for lunch was stunning. There was a big long shared table, and huge timber and glass windows that took in the breathtaking view of the ocean. We sat with a big group of friends, all couples and really lovely to talk to. We were chatting about life and swapping some funny stories. I noticed Hannes seemed quiet. Also, he was drinking really fast. I was a few sips into mine and he asked if I wanted another one. His was already empty so he made his way back to the bar. After lunch Hannes suggested we go outside and look at the view, which really was beautiful. I was busy talking – how unusual – and I looked over to Hannes but he was out of sight. He called my name – he was down on one knee.

Holy shit, I was getting proposed to! I had seen this a thousand times in films but didn't quite understand that it was happening to me. Hannes looked so handsome, I could tell he was nervous. While he was down on one knee, he was trying to unwrap something in his pocket.

'Tania, I love you, will you be my wife and marry me?'

I was quiet maybe for the first time in my life, I was just processing the moment.

I get down on one knee, then two.

Thinking about this image, the whole venue through the big open windows looking at this couple that looked to both be kneeling and facing each other – were they thinking, what is going on here?

I was just so shocked, even though I knew we were in love and I wanted to marry Hannes.

I ask if that is a real ring while I hold my hand out to see.

Hannes smiles and nods while shaking, he tries to put it on my finger.

I stare at it. It's stunning, an antique from the 1950s, and the diamonds just sparkle so much in the natural light; it gleams.

'Did you ask my parents?'

Hannes smiles again, 'Yes, I asked them both over Christmas.'

'Oh my god, you asked my parents and that's a real ring.'

'Tania, you haven't answered my question yet.'

I grab him and kiss him and say, 'Yes! Yes, of course I will marry you!'

We are both crying tears of happiness, I'm still in a little shock and amazement that this is happening. I feel so full of love for Hannes, for the moment, for life – it's a beautiful feeling.

We can't stop smiling, I am staring at the ring telling him how much I love it, did he pick it by himself? He says yes beaming with pride, that he did a good job, it's obvious, I am so happy. We kiss and cuddle some more. Both with the biggest grins, some random people ask to come over and take our photo as they were so happy for us. Hannes and I are still on cloud nine so agree to be in some complete stranger's holiday pictures.

We walk back into the venue holding hands and there is a cheer from the table. The girls rush over to look at the ring and congratulate me, the men go and pat Hannes on the back and shake his hand. One says, 'I told them you were about to pop the question; you had that look all over your face and were downing the beers quicker than anyone at the table!' We all laugh, it felt good. This would be one of my favourite moments of all time, thinking about it forever puts a smile on my face. I look at Hannes, 'You did so well. How I didn't find out is amazing.' He smiles and agrees.

MY VERY FIRST EURO TRIP

In the European summer of 2016, Hannes and I planned our very first trip to Europe. Not just our first trip there together, my first trip there ever. We started in Germany where I would meet his whole family. I had met his parents the previous summer in Australia, so I already knew I loved them. But there were his siblings and their partners and kids, aunts and uncles and cousins.

We arrived close to midnight. I wasn't sure if we were going to catch up that night or the next day. Hannes informed me that his family wouldn't miss a chance to meet us the night we arrived. We walked into a celebration! It wasn't just his siblings, it was extended family too. I was greeted by his aunty delivering me a glass of champagne on a silver tray, and all his nieces and nephews had made a huge banner metres in length that said 'WELCOME!' with an Australian flag and a German one painted on the sign, I was blown away by it all. Hannes said because we got engaged it was a bit of a celebration of sorts too. It was incredible, I felt like I was famous. I instantly knew Hannes' family accepted me and his engagement to a girl in Australia, and I was thrilled.

We spent the next week in his home village. I got tours all around town, in the car or on the back of the Vespa to all the surrounding villages, it really was a dream come true. Not only had I made it to Europe, I was marrying a German, so this would be a regular part of our future life together. I met all Hannes' friends and their families, and everyone was just lovely. One thing I noticed is even when they said they didn't speak English, they spoke it very well. Enough so we could have a conversation. One thing I was asked time and time again, was to slow down when speaking. I get excited easily and if I am drinking, it just adds another layer of excitement to my stories, which makes me talk quicker than usual.

One night we were at his aunty and uncle's having dinner with the family. They pride themselves on being excellent hosts. There was never once a moment when my beer or wine glass was half empty. This makes it extremely difficult to work out exactly how much one is consuming. Hannes' Mum had told me about how she learnt English through The Beatles, so I connected with Hannes' parents through music. Hannes told me how much his aunty and uncle like music too, so boom, I was on. I had my playlist set up and playing The Beatles, The Eagles, The Animals and Cat Stevens, we were playing it all. Hannes and I kicked on with them till close to 3am, the four of us dancing and singing together. I could have sworn there was a moment when they were speaking perfect English and I was speaking fluent German. Champagne and music were a marvellous combination.

The next part of our Euro trip was an epic road trip in Hannes' brother's car to visit my extended family, my Deda's brothers and sisters, in Montenegro – family I had never met. We had no accommodation booked, we were just driving across not just states but countries. It was one of the most wonderful experiences of my life. It was summer in Europe, I was freshly engaged, in love and on an adventure. I honestly thought, life can't get better than this. We would stop in a country like Austria just for the night. After checking in at a hotel, we'd jump into the lake, lie in the sun, then dry off and wander. I have always loved the idea of being somewhere I have never been before, somewhere I may never go again. It's exciting and I don't think I had ever felt so free. Then next morning we would get up and do it all again, capital cities, small coastal towns, we experienced such stunning wonders of the world, including Plitvice Lakes. Plitvice Lakes is a national park in Croatia, full of lakes joined by waterfalls that extend to limestone canyons. We spent the whole day exploring and although you can't actually swim in the water, as they want to keep it pristine, the clear blue water looks as though it's a painting; the clarity was perfect.

We arrived in Bar, Montenegro for the first planned catch-up. We had been invited to Mum's cousin's house for lunch. Hannes and I both tell this story differently. It was close to lunch time and we weren't meeting them till 4pm. We had spent a bit of time swimming and, as I like to eat, I suggested we grab something for lunch, something small – a pizza and salad to share. Hannes disagreed completely. He said we were going to meet my family, who we couldn't communicate with. This was true, they spoke no English apart from your basics and Hannes was trying to explain to me they will speak to us through our stomachs, communicate via cooking. I knew this would no doubt be the case, but I didn't want to rock up starving to relatives I had never met in another country. Hannes said, they are family, it will be fine. I won the battle of will we or won't we get lunch, just something small to tide us over.

On our way to the house, we couldn't put the address we had in the car's navigator, and Google Maps also wasn't working. We tried calling my cousin, but she couldn't speak English and I couldn't speak Serbian. It was time to call my mum to get her to call them to translate. We were a little screwed. We ended up stopping at a corner store and the owner directed us up a hill. We were completely lost. We ended up on a property that was off the main road. A man came out in a filthy off-white singlet and dress pants; he had the same style as my Deda. We tried to explain that we were lost and could he direct us to the address in my phone. He told us he spoke no English. Hannes with a quick idea asked if he could speak German. The man suddenly called out and his daughter appeared, turns out the young girl spoke German. She explained to her father where we needed to go. He then called my cousins and got directions for us, which he then translated to his daughter, who then told Hannes and so forth. It was fucking hilarious. This family didn't even know us and went so far out of their way to help. The whole episode must have taken at least half an hour.

When we finally rocked up it was instant love. We couldn't speak the same language, but we laughed, hugged and even cried, it was wonderful. This family that I didn't even know I had welcomed us with such open arms, it was just amazing. You could tell we were related as all three daughters were tall, tanned and had dark brown hair and features like me. Hannes couldn't get over how similar we all looked even though we lived in different parts of the world. Of course Hannes was correct about the food. They'd cooked a five-course meal of all my favourite Serbian dishes, and then some, plus Nutella crêpes to top it off. We were in heaven. After the late lunch and dinner, we followed them in our car, so we knew where our hotel was, and caught up with them again over the next few days. Bar is a beautiful coastal town filled with amazing people. The rest of our Europe trip continued like that. We met more extended family, who just adored us.

There is a lot that I now understand about my family, from meeting my extended family from my Deda's side, his younger sisters and brothers; the youngest has a 20-year age gap with my grandfather. I felt so much love and pride for these people I didn't even know, but it didn't feel like that, it felt like home. Even with the language barrier.

The time we spent together was treasured. It's quite funny as, before he died, my granddad thought it was easier to tell his family that Hannes and I were married. They are pretty traditional there and if you live together you should be married, so even though we were newly engaged, to them we were freshly married. Due to the language barrier I wasn't able to correct them, so we just rolled with it.

One of the moments that really touched me was how happy they all were with nothing in comparison to how we live at home. The more we travelled through this part of the world, the more that became clear. From Bar, we'd driven to Berane, a few hours inland from the coast, to visit family who lived in this area. One day, when I returned to our hotel from a run, Hannes was sitting in the lobby with a relative. He was a cousin of my mother's. He drove an ambulance for a living and had come to take us out for the afternoon and spend time with him and his family. He was married to a beautiful woman and they had four daughters: a teenager, a 7-year-old, a 5-year-old and a 6-month-old baby. Their house was one level, it looked to only be a few bedrooms. It was filled with that much warmth and love. You felt it as soon as you entered. We had cheese strudel, black coffee and fresh seasonal fruit. While we were eating, they brought out family photo albums. The last time they saw my mum in their home town, she was my age.

They had photos of them together and it made them so proud to show me. Seeing photos of my mum with her relatives in a town across the oceans made me feel so happy about who I was and my heritage. They took us for a big walking tour around Berane. All the buildings looked as though they had stood the test of time. There's a long winding river named the Lim that runs down from the peak of the mountains. We made our way to the top of a lookout over the town, we just stood there taking it all in. Then we made our way back down, to stroll through the cobblestoned Corso. This is where all the action is: cafés, bars and shops. Along the way we played games with the girls and even though we couldn't really speak the same words, the conversation flowed the whole afternoon. Laughing and communicating without a common language is a wonderful thing to experience.

We sat at a café where a summer festival had been set up. There was a band and singers on a big stage, we had prime real estate to watch the world go by. We started with some short black coffees, and the girls all getting a can of Coke and an ice-cream. We sat and enjoyed the live music for hours, drinking 50-cent cold beers and enjoying the company and the experience. There were many families and young friends doing just as we were. Hannes got all the girls a balloon and the joy that it brought them was something else. I don't think I have ever seen kids play with a balloon on a stick for hours with the biggest smiles on their faces and warm laughter escaping their lips. They were having a ball and it was a safe environment, they could run off and play with other kids and dance around, with parents keeping one eye on the band and one eye on the children. Songs started that I can only imagine in Australia would be the equivalent to John Farnham's 'You're the Voice' or Daryl Braithwaite's 'Horses' with everyone knowing the lyrics and singing at the top of their lungs.

Hannes fixed up the bill and the family were overwhelmed by our generosity – they were the ones that were meant to treat us. We explained they had been such wonderful hosts all day and it was our way of saying thank you. The bill wasn't even 30 Euros for hours and hours of drinks and snacks. In that moment I just knew that these people didn't have much, but what they did have was big hearts and so much kindness. They may possibly be the happiest family I have ever met to this day. They walked us home and we said our goodbyes. I will always cherish the time we spent together, with all my relatives.

THE YEAR THAT WAS

My relationship with my mum was extremely close, as I am sure you've gathered by now. I spoke to her at least daily. I liked to call her on my way to work, she would tell me what was happening on *Sunrise*, the morning show, and what the Melbourne weather was doing that day; even though I can get the weather and news in an instant, I enjoyed our daily tradition of Mum updating me. I wanted to see how she was sleeping, tell her stories or give her updates, we could discuss the books we were reading, just the usual morning chit-chat.

Mum had been complaining of pain in her back, I had noticed over the last few weeks, even months. She was in a great deal of radiating pain and she couldn't explain why or where it had been building from. This had become the hot topic of our conversation. I had grown really worried as during our morning chats, I could tell Mum was in pain. She had seen a doctor, but they couldn't explain it. She ended up getting cortisone injections to help ease the pain in the area until a specialist could work out what was triggering it. Mum had a high pain threshold, but something wasn't right.

Us kids all arrived for Serbian Christmas in Sydney, we had Hannes' brother and his girlfriend visiting at the time. We were showing them not just the sights of Melbourne but Sydney too. Over Christmas, it was as always a beautiful time together. We'd started the tradition of seeing my dad and his sisters on the Serbian Christmas Eve and we spent Christmas Day with the Kumovi. The thing was though, Mum had started using a walking stick to get around. You could see the pain she was suffering in her face, something serious was going on and we needed answers. As always, Mum the champion, soldiered on and tried to play it down. She needed to rest more than usual and was having trouble getting up and down from a seat. As always, we enjoyed this time together, but more so now than just as an annual event – living in different states, it was harder to all get together. I flew to Sydney all the time to see Mum, but when we were all together, it was such a treat.

At the start of February, I called Mum on the way to work as usual. When she answered, she was panicked. I asked her what was wrong and she told me she couldn't move; she was lying on her bed in excruciating pain. She had called an ambulance. A friend from her building was waiting with her until it arrived. I told her I would call the kids and let them know and for her to call me as soon as she made it to the hospital.

FUCK! Now I was in a panic, I called Dana and Mike and explained what had happened, we didn't have any updates, but Mum was going to hospital. I spoke to work and explained something was going on with my mum and I needed to be ready to fly up the next day. I have been lucky, as the places I have worked have always been very understanding when it comes to putting family first.

On the third of February, Mum got her scan results. Her breast cancer was back, it had become metastatic cancer also known as secondary cancer. The cancer had spread and had eaten through Mum's vertebrae causing collapse. No wonder Mum was in so much pain – a tumour had eaten through her vertebrae and fucking collapsed her spine. She couldn't walk or move, she needed to be rushed in to major surgery.

You know when you have a feeling, deep down in the pit of your stomach? It could be regarding anything. It's there and you can't shake it, you feel it building and instead of focusing on it, you push it down further, ignore it and pray to god it goes away? This whole episode brought us back to Mum having cancer. She had been in remission for a couple of years now and things seemed to be looking up. That feeling that I couldn't shake was dread because deep down cancer is a fucking menace. It preys on people, it is not biased about who – it will take down anyone in its path. This time it had its evil claws set on my mum again. The feeling that washes over you when you get this news is heartbreak, anger, grief, pain, sadness then a big FUCK YOU to the world and everyone in it. 'It's not fair' are words that I would often use. It's not fucking fair, why can't she have a break, why can't she just have a good year and enjoy herself and her health? It shatters your world and everything in it.

Mum had an operation that entailed eight hours' worth of surgery. She had 16 screws and two rods put into her back and the tumours became infused almost in a little box of vertebrae. Due to it being so close to the nerves, they couldn't just remove it while they were operating. It couldn't be cut out. Once Mum got strong enough from her back operation, she would begin radiotherapy for the second time in the last few years.

I stayed with Mum while she healed. In true Mum style she got stronger and a bit more like herself every day. It was going to be a long road to recovery again, but this time they couldn't remove the cancer. They could shrink it and it would need a watchful eye on it as cancer gets smart and as soon as the cells shift and morph it can travel. Mum stayed in hospital till the twenty-first of February, every day doing physio and trying to practise walking and sitting and moving with the new added features in her back. It was hard to see Mum so uncomfortable and defeated, but of course she held her head up high as that's what she does. When I got her home, she was so happy to be back in her own bed.

Less than a month later was our engagement party in Manly. Slowly but surely, Mum got even stronger every day and she was able to make it. To date this was one of the most important events in my life. A hundred of our nearest and dearest were there. Hannes' parents flew over, and Stefan, Hannes' brother, surprised us by showing up too, with nothing more than a backpack, just to join the celebration. He said he couldn't miss a party with all his favourite Aussies who he'd met when he'd come over and spent the Christmas before with us, and we all loved him. It was so special for him to be there. And Mum. Mum was there, she made it. She couldn't dance, which broke her heart and mine, but she could be present, standing and enjoying the moment by my side. This was huge, just a month prior she couldn't even walk, and to have her there overwhelmed me with happiness. When I was giving my speech, I told everyone just that as I burst into tears, how much it meant to have everyone there but most importantly my mum. She got a big cheer from the crowd and everyone knew the significance of that moment.

MUMMA'S BIRTHDAY BASH

We had decided after the engagement we were going to throw a big party for Mum's 65th birthday. We wanted to invite 40 of her closest friends and family, have a celebration for her because why not? After the C bomb news we really didn't need an excuse to have a party for Mum. She loved hosting parties for us as kids and it was a pleasure to return the favour. Picture this: we had a grazing platter that was about four metres long, with customer-made cakes, cheeses from all over the globe, meats from Spain and Italy, pâté, dips and fruit, as well as sweets galore, freshly baked baguettes, and just when no one could fit in any more food, we ordered late-night pizzas from the best pizza place on the Northern Beaches because there is always room for pizza.

We had music blasting, cocktails flowing and a fully stocked bar. Mum even got her make-up done for the party which was a real treat. Mum felt like a rock star and was showered with love. My mum was a popular woman. It felt good to make her feel special. The older I get the more I really believe you should celebrate birthdays; they are a day to celebrate you and all you have achieved. The older you get, the wiser you become, so they say, and Mum was the prime example of this.

Along with the highs came the lows, and shortly after Mum's birthday, her latest scan results came with a blow we had all been dreading. We thought things had been good, Mum had reacted well to all treatment, she seemed like she had more energy and was doing all the right things; we were being positive as that is how we had taught ourselves to be. But all the positive vibes in the world couldn't help us. Mum's breast cancer had spread again, this time to her lungs. From what we had learnt from the previous time, as it was breast cancer that had spread to an organ, they would not be able to operate. So here we were, picking up the broken pieces and telling ourselves it was going to be okay and we would be there for Mum. Of course Mum was determined as always to beat it, she refused to give up. If anything, she would hold back how she really felt, her tears, her anger, all just to protect her children. Her positive energy could be felt from miles away. Mum did not want to be a victim of the C word, and we had to once again catch our breath, cry, hold back tears, cry some more, and shake it off and get ready for round three.

Mum had been on an oral chemotherapy, in tablet form, which is a much milder dose after her back operation; we had learnt it'd stopped working after a course of a few months. What happens with cancer from witnessing it first-hand with Mum, is the cells get smart, so smart in fact, you need to be one step ahead. There was a pattern with this cancer treatment. For Mum's three-month scans it mostly seemed to be keeping things at bay. If you squinted enough at the CT scan, the tumours seemed to be shrinking by a millimetre or there was no new growth, but by her six-month scans, things started to shift, that feeling was back in your guts and you tried to push it away, but you were always wary and had a negative feeling about the results, and time and time again traumatically this theory was proven right by the results each scan gave us. Mum was starting a trial drug for treatment; we wouldn't know this at the time, but it would be the first of many.

A VERY GERMAN WEDDING

Hannes and I planned to get married in Germany. It was my suggestion as Hannes chose to live in Australia with me and I thought this would be something special for him and for us, sharing the moment with all his family.

We kept the guest list tight from the Australian side. The engagement was a celebration for everyone to be part of our special day as we knew a destination wedding was a huge ask. I fell in love with a German, and most of my crew knew this would be on the horizon.

My mum and sister were doing a Euro trip of their own visiting Croatia, Serbia, Italy and most importantly, Paris, my mum's favourite place in the world, which she had never been to. It fills me with love that Dana got to experience this time with Mum, that they got to go together. Mum based her style and her apartment, almost her way of life, on being chic and French. She just loved the idea of French women having so much elegance and class about them. For her, there was something about how they carried themselves.

Keka was also making the wedding. It makes me so happy to have shared that moment with her. She had her birthday at the same time and included a cruise on her trip, and as it was her 70th she treated herself to business class flights. Meanwhile, she'd made friends with her travel agent, who she said was the sweetest guy, and whose partner worked for Emirates. They ended up upgrading her return flight to first class as a surprise! When I ask what her favourite part of the trip was, she says the upgrade, then quickly changes it to the wedding, but we all know a first-class upgrade would be the ultimate.

Keka also did the most unbelievable thing – she upgraded Mum to business. It was the most amazing gesture and meant the world to all of us, including Mum. Since Mum had had that big back operation earlier in the year, it was a miracle she could even make the wedding and not only that but travel the world, and my aunty, Mum's ex-sister-in-law, shouted her the upgrade so she could do it in style and comfort.

My Kuma also came, and she is the best travel buddy ever, so easy. Throw her in a crowd and she will have fun. We were up one night at Stefan's 40th birthday party, dancing to Johnny Cash's 'Walk the Line' at 5am. There aren't many godmothers that can do that, let me tell you, and it just brought us all even closer. My brother also made the wedding with his partner and in true Michael form, he had five days to do the trip, including the Buck's night, and was completing his first ever marathon two days before the wedding. When he called to tell me, he said, please don't get mad, but this is what I am doing. I told him I am used to him being random and as long as his legs can dance and he can enjoy himself after that, it's absolutely fine by me.

Planning a wedding in a country you don't speak the language of is a wild mission, I take my hat off to anyone who has done it before because you know what you deserve? A gold fucking star. The stress is next level and there's so much added pressure. Good news is, if you pull it off, you win points with all your new European extended family, so that's a plus, and everyone who makes the trip gets to enjoy all that comes with a German wedding sensation.

On our first trip together to Germany, when I met his family for the first time, we went to a few venues and locked in the one we both liked the most that day. I liked the idea that they would do a lot of the work on the day, save us running around. We only arrived 10 days before the wedding and 10 days goes fast when you have a 90-person event to plan which is also meant to be up there with the biggest day of your life.

Being a control freak and a planner at the best of times added a few extra layers of being overwhelmed.

The venue was amazing. It was a fancy restaurant on a golf course surrounded by pine trees that made it look as though we were in the Black Forest, which wasn't that far away. Our wedding was in a wooden hut, but a very flash modern wooden hut. The walls were covered in cuckoo clocks and stuffed local animals like foxes, and deer horns. It had a real presence – you were greeted by a giant taxidermy black bear, which Hannes laughed at because there are no bears in Germany, but the Aussies didn't need to know that. The venue coordinator was lovely and had excellent English, which was another reason that swayed us.

The weather was terrible leading up to the wedding. Something I need to do to Zen out and calm the fuck down is exercise, but the weather was so bad that I couldn't. Now, leading up to my wedding, I needed to get my rig in check. I was about to be a bride, I needed to be looking my best. The thing is, in Germany, the diet consists of bread, potatoes, meat and beer. Pre wedding, I was carb loading! There was not a salad in sight. At home it would be a different story. Don't get me wrong, I love those things very much. I am a beer girl through and through, but when it's raining and you're with family all you do is drink and eat. I also wasn't getting a moment to myself and the pressure was building.

My dad had also arrived. Look, yes, I had a father to walk me down the aisle, but at the time, stress levels were high. My dad had recently discovered Facebook. His first post was:

> Retired, single man, 3 grown-up children, ready
> to travel.

I got sent that many screenshots from family and friends asking me whether I'd seen it. Did he think it was Tinder!? Of course my dad had a status update that made out he was on a dating app for the youth. God help us all.

It's lucky my Kuma arrived the same time as my dad as she could tell I was getting stressed and he was not helping. Let me set the scene.

My dad for his first ever trip to Europe had flown himself business class, yet had not given me a dime towards my wedding. The first wedding of one of his children. To put it in perspective, when my parents got married, they had 500 guests, and who do you think paid for it? Their fathers.

Originally, he wasn't going to make the wedding as he didn't have any money. Surprise, surprise! Hannes' dad heard this news and offered to pay for his flight, he knew my dad couldn't miss his daughter's wedding. My dad ended up getting his inheritance from my grandma; the house sold just before the wedding, so he'd come into some cash at the perfect time.

When we picked him up from the airport, he was excited. It was a big deal, his first flight to Europe, not to mention business class being the way he'd travelled. He had a new tracksuit, new iPad, new bag, new shoes. Bloke was kitted out.

We arrived at Hannes' parents' house where they had prepared a lovely lunch for us all, with wines to match. It was a special occasion and Hannes' parents were so proud. Dana and Mum wouldn't arrive for a few days. After lunch, my dad thought it was the perfect opportunity to tell us that he'd purchased a 22-wheel three-bedroom caravan, not just any caravan, but the most top-notch one on the market. I was puzzled by this statement, as my dad had only just received his inheritance and would be travelling overseas for three months. And he had gone and spent 80 percent of his money on a caravan, which he didn't even have a truck or ute to transport?

Plus, he had clearly said he didn't have money to make the wedding, so now to fly business class as well as buy a house on wheels, when he'd been living with my grandma and the house had sold. The bloke didn't have anywhere to live and now was bragging.

The final straw was when he started showing Hannes photos of some bird from his Facebook, who he claimed was his girlfriend. She was young and fit, but the punchline is, she wasn't real, she was a scam. Here we all are, sitting around the table after this delicious lunch and Dad is pulling out his phone, not only showing photos of her face but fucking topless photos. I was about to kill the guy. Hannes was in so much shock.

I told Dad, once in a very soft but stern tone, if I saw his phone out one more time and he showed one more photo of a blonde bimbo from the internet, he would not be walking me down the aisle. I was furious. For me to even have Dad at the wedding was a huge fucking step. I was on the fence about having him there as I just knew he would do something embarrassing, and here we were on day one, and he's bragging about his new wheels, his new girlfriend, the expensive flight and all the champagne he'd had on it. I was ready to kill him; if Kuma wasn't there to hold me back, I may well have.

We decided to get married in Hannes' local church. The church is old and beautiful and has a lot of history with Hannes and his family, so I thought having it there was a nice way to honour his family's traditions and I knew everyone making the trip would love it. Now, there were a few things that popped up during the planning process. Don't get me wrong, I love my husband, but boy I could have strangled him. It's quite common in European churches to have a booklet during the wedding service. You do not have to, but it's an option. Hannes' mum had mentioned we could have one if we wanted. I said flat-out no as it was just another thing I would have to organise, and the list was piling up of things to do. When we had our sit-down with the priest, he was quite modern and we spoke about having the service half in English and half in German so everyone could understand. He loves music so we were able to incorporate songs I gave him. Music being a big part of our lives, it was important to have some played even during the church service. Leon Bridges' 'The River', Paper Kites' 'Bloom' and an instrumental version of Elvis' 'Can't Help Falling in Love' would be played by Hannes' father and uncle on guitar and saxophone as I was walking down the aisle. The thought of it made me extremely happy. While running through a few things with the priest, he asked if we would have a church booklet. He said we didn't have to, but it was a nice touch. On the spot Hannes said of course we would have one. I glared at him – Hannes, we had a deal, no church booklets – but Hannes refused to make eye contact. Hannes' dad made it his job to organise it, which we were very thankful for, but every night, I would hear my name.

'Tania! Tania,' he would call, and I would go and see what was needed. He wanted to run through the design, the images, the poems, the prayers, the music, more readings, more songs. It was so lovely he wanted to do it, but Hannes did not help with one part of this booklet that I'd been helping his dad design for five nights in a row.

'Hannes, if there is one more song in our wedding, it's going to turn into a musical! No more songs.'

It just kept getting out of control. Of course, it turned out perfectly, but Hannes wasn't involved in one conversation regarding it. Go figure, the bloke that wanted it.

On the day we had to organise our cake, Hannes' mum took me to the best cake shop of all the nearby villages. I had a good idea of what I wanted: a six-tiered semi-naked layered cake. However, I got two giant love hearts that were on one level in pink icing. It was the only design in the book that looked wedding-like, but it had all these green icing leaves in the picture. I asked whether they could cancel the green leaves, which Hannes' mum was translating, and just have the two big hearts. The complete opposite of any wedding cake I had visualised for my own wedding, but what do you do! This was the option and we could make it work. We decided on a black forest cake, given our proximity to the real thing. I went to pay for the cake in advance, so it'd be one less thing I had to worry about. We also needed to pick up fresh pretzels as it was tradition for after the church service to have champagne and pretzels under the trees nearby. Hannes was trying to explain to me it's a small village and we don't pay in advance, we pay on the day. I was trying to explain without sounding like a bridezilla, that I was going to be a little too fucking busy on my wedding day to pick up 100 pretzels and a double love heart wedding cake. Hannes kept insisting and then finally his mum, who is the best mother-in-law in the world, said she would sort everything out for us, and so she did. Thank you to my mother-in-law for saving the day!

The other tradition we thought we would uphold is a Buck's and Hen's while we were there. This was organised by the Germans and will go down as one of the best experiences of my life.

For the Hen's, us girls piled into a minivan where we enjoyed a schnapps on the way to a property in the Black Forest where all kinds of activities were set up. Something like this would never work in Australia due to safety rules, but in Germany, anything goes. We were split into teams and played games and while we played, we drank beers and ciders at the open bar. For the first game, we dressed up in bright yellow safety jumpsuits and had to ride a tiny wooden bike down a hill and stop before an electric fence, I kid you not. It was a relay, so we were competing against the other team. There were a few epic stacks, me included. I got a grass burn from rolling sideways off the bike before I reached the fence and a scratch on my elbow that's visible in all my wedding photos, which makes me laugh to this day. We did hammer throwing, we also did human foosball where we had to climb over this wall into a pen and hold onto the wood and plastic rack in front of us which turned us into the pieces in the game to stop the ball going past. Who knew my girlfriends were so competitive? There was also laser-tag shooting – turns out Kuma is a gun when it comes to target practice! Finally, we all got to ride a bucking bull. I was really trying to beat the top score and did smoke it, but also kind of cheated by hooking my long legs around part of the bull, which caused a bruise about as big as my hand to form on the back of my knee – it was the biggest bruise I have ever had in my life. Thank god my dress was floor-length.

Afterwards we had the best feast and made our way to a cocktail bar and from there ended up at a nightclub called Club OK; if someone asked us what it was like, we'd definitely say it was okay. We got that much attention and must have stood out like sore thumbs, the biggest group of Aussies that this small town had ever seen. One of the highlights was when Elissa and I were trying to make our way to the bathroom and somehow ended up in a room on a dance floor where everyone was line dancing. This day was something else; a quick boot-scoot and off to the bathroom because really, we couldn't help but join in.

When I asked the boys how the Buck's was, it was something very similar – activities on a farm with an open bar, lots of food, and they ended up at a venue called One Night in Paris. The German groomsmen wanted to compete with the Aussies when they heard they'd been to Hannes' Buck's night at a strip club in Melbourne. If you have been to this strip club, you would know you're in for a real treat, even if it's not your Buck's. The place the Germans took the boys to, well, to this day when they describe the place, they are horrified. It didn't seem like a strip club, more like a house with a stage show, and I will leave it at that. A for effort, such a laugh all round and memories that will make them giggle and cringe for years to come.

I heard through the grapevine my dad had once again been carrying on, telling all my mates he was dating some woman he'd met on Facebook. He was going to see her in Brisbane where she lived but was waiting for her divorce to go through. Dad told all my boys that this bird drove a Ferrari and was really into him, that she sent topless photos and all. Even after I had spoken to Dad, he continued showing photos of his fake girlfriend from the internet to my mates at the Buck's and he explained all she wanted from him in return was iTunes gift cards. The boys said, 'Come on, David, surely you are not that stupid!? She's fake! She's trying to have you on!' But of course my dad once again believed he was right. I was furious. To think he came to my wedding as an excuse to brag and show off, because he certainly didn't get involved with any of the activities, he just played on his phone obsessing over Facebook and god knows what dating sites. It's amazing after all these years, my dad can still embarrass himself like that, you'd think the bloke would have learnt by now.

The night before the wedding we planned to have a practice run at the church, just the groomsmen, my bridesmaids, Hannes and I, very simple, so we all knew what we were doing on the day. This was all new to me so I wanted to make sure everything went according to plan.

I had three bridesmaids, Dana, Elissa and Lucy, and we were a little delayed getting there as we'd been to see the biggest waterfall around and have lunch in a town about an hour away on the train. We missed the train coming back. When we arrived, we went straight to the church.

When we got there, I asked Hannes where the groomsmen were.

Hannes responded that they were busy, they had kids and couldn't make it.

I said that seems strange as the wedding is tomorrow, surely they could have made it work. It was 6pm and no one was working.

He told me they were busy.

By this stage, I was pretty pissed off. Not only was I overwhelmed by the fact that our wedding day was the following day, there was just a lot going on. My dress had lost some beading from transporting it across the globe, it was heavy silk and the top layer and back were completely beaded. It was stunning, but I was worried, as when I'd tried it on the day before, I lost some beads and it looked like more were going to come apart. I also had to check after my diet of no exercise and beer, beer, meat and pretzels whether the bloody thing even fit. Lucky stress is a godsend and I hadn't put on any weight, it still fit like a glove.

Yet here we are in the church, and I am pissed off at my almost husband.

He tells me, 'How is it so hard? Lucy walks in, Elissa walks in, Dana walks in and then you walk in.'

The girls are standing there. Now my blood is boiling.

'Hannes, what the fuck! I can't believe you forgot to tell the groomsmen. It would have been nice if the bridesmaids met the person they were partnered up with for the day, and honestly I don't think it was too much to ask.'

'Tania, don't swear in the church.'

'Hannes, you are doing my head in! My stress is running really fucking high, I haven't asked you to do one fucking thing. We are leaving, I have got so much to do.'

We bail. All the Aussies are staying in the two hotels in town. We walk Dana and Lucy to theirs and I tell them I will see them soon. I had a big dinner planned at their hotel for my family and friends from Australia.

I am walking Elissa back to her hotel, and a car drives past just as we cross from the church. It's a car with not one, but all three fucking groomsmen. They weren't working or busy, they'd just been hanging out together. Hannes hadn't even asked them.

They all wave and yell out the window, 'See you tomorrow!'

Elissa looks at me and says, 'Take some deep breaths.'

It's 6.45pm by the time I'm walking home. The dinner is at 8pm, and I still need to wash my hair and pack my bag as I am staying the night with my mum and sister. Keeping with tradition, I wouldn't see Hannes till the wedding.

I also had to pack his cute present of socks, in case he got cold feet, mints for kissable breath, Lifesavers in case he needed one on the day and a candy ring as a back-up if he misplaced the real one. Because even though I know I can be a bitch under pressure, I am very thoughtful. I am so rushed and trying to run out the door and Hannes wants me to meet the driver and have a beer with them. I tell them politely, thank you, but I need to hurry to get to the dinner with the 24 Australians waiting for me. Hannes tells me he will drive me, but it's only a 10-minute walk, and I needed it to calm down.

I am nearly at the restaurant but I stop before I go inside. Elissa calls and asks if I am okay and says she'll come out and get me. I am okay, I don't want to make out I am that dramatic. I can't explain how I felt in this moment. So overwhelmed, but not due to the stress of the wedding the next day or Hannes. I wasn't going to call off the wedding over the groomsmen. No, it was because so many people I loved, my nearest and dearest, were there. I couldn't invite everyone and of course some couldn't make it – we did pick a whole other country to marry in – but I was just so overwhelmed. I could really feel the love, it's the night before my wedding, everyone is waiting for me to come to dinner. Amazing friends that have been part of my life for a very long time, my Keka, my Kuma, my brother and his girlfriend, my sister, my dad, and the main reason was my mum.

My mum had come all the way across the world living with cancer. Not only had she had that huge back operation earlier that year, her breast cancer had spread to her lungs, and despite all the odds, she was there for me. Some of the people had never even been to Europe before or hadn't even been on a plane and they were there for me. I was so overwhelmed with happiness and love, all I could do was cry. Elissa came out and gave me the biggest hug and told me they were all waiting for the guest of honour. It was an incredibly strong and powerful feeling that came over me. I couldn't help but think how can I be worthy of this much joy, so much love, it was a beautiful thing. Dinner was a success. My thanks go to Fergie who stayed up fixing the beading on my dress while I stayed up drinking red wine till at least 1am with the last ones standing. It was the perfect way to de-stress and unwind before the big day.

The wedding was a success, too. It was the first sunny day we had seen in weeks, and the temperature was perfect. The day went as planned, and my dress I loved just as much as the day I found it. Sure, I would have loved more sleep instead of getting my make-up done at 8am even though the wedding didn't start till 3pm, but this was the only time they could do. And yes, I was a tad hung-over on my wedding day, but I wouldn't have expected anything less from myself.

Everyone looked stunning, even though my mum said the make-up artist was a little heavy-handed on her eye make-up and she felt as though she looked like a tranny. We assured her she looked stunning. There was so much love in the air.

I entered the church to 'Can't Help Falling in Love' performed by Hannes' dad and uncle and it was such a special moment. My long silk dress, which had a trail, glided along the floor. It was backless, and the top of the dress came down in a cowl neck detail, the beads matched the colour of the dress. At that moment with all eyes on me, I honestly felt as though I had stepped into my very own fairy tale.

When I walked down the aisle and saw Hannes, he was tearing up. The feeling I had was indescribable. I was so happy and everything felt so perfect in that moment. He looked so handsome in his charcoal suit, with his crisp white shirt, white pocket square, a pink rose pinned to his lapel.

He told me I looked stunning through glassy eyes and a moment later asked me, 'Does my hair look okay?' because when we go to a wedding, I like his hair a bit slicker, brushed down to one side. He nailed it. He also told me he wanted to kiss me, but we didn't know if we were allowed yet. We just stood holding hands grinning like two Cheshire cats the whole service.

The wedding was the ultimate day. We mixed German traditions with Australian traditions, which kept everyone entertained. The DJ I had organised was just fantastic, he and I had been swapping music for months leading up to the wedding. To this day we keep in touch. Between the entrée and the main, Mum started a conga line which included almost all 90 wedding guests. I have never seen that many people dancing so early at a wedding and I loved that our wedding was the one that did it. Hannes told me it was German tradition that the bride and groom stay till the sun comes up. I didn't believe this at first, but when I asked the venue what time we had to leave, they just said as long as guests were done by the next morning, it was fine. They had to set up an event at 11am. Our wedding was still going at 6.30am when I told Hannes we would need to start getting people to leave. There was full service and by 3am everyone was drinking from Steins, and the midnight cheese platter went down an absolute treat. We didn't even do our first dance till after midnight, no one wanted to leave and the celebrations just kept going.

At one stage I had run off to the bathroom and when I came back, all the lights were off, the dance floor was lit by everyone holding just a tea light candle, and suddenly 'I Will Always Love You' by Whitney Houston started playing and a circle had formed. What the heck was going on? Was this another German tradition? Hannes signalled for me to come over. We were dancing in this circle lit by tea light candles and I was laughing so hard, thinking this is by far the strangest thing I have ever seen. When I caught Lucy's and the girls' eyes, they were in stitches. This is a moment in time that has no photographic proof but is embedded in my mind, and as romantic as the DJ and Hannes thought it was, I was cracking up! It was bloody hilarious.

The wedding went down as a 13-hour reception. One of the boys googled it and reckons it would have gone down in the *Guinness Book of World Records* as one of the longest weddings going. I think I got to bed about 9am. We had heard that the majority of couples on their wedding night do not have sex as they are mentally and physically drained from the day, and as cooked as we were after a 13-hour dance party, Hannes made sure the odds were in our favour and we didn't become a statistic against sex on the wedding night. Well-played, Lover Boy!

THE MANYMOON

What better way to celebrate a destination wedding than a manymoon with your mates that made the trip. See, I tried to sell this idea to Hannes. Do not get me wrong, he loves our friends, but he couldn't quite understand why I wanted them to come on our honeymoon.

'Not the whole thing,' I would tell him, 'just to Portugal. Three nights in Lisbon, three nights in Lagos. Then you and I can get all romantic in Greece afterwards and I promise you can have me all to yourself.'

The first part of the honeymoon was dubbed the manymoon. It was just perfect! There aren't many times in your adult life you will be away with your best mates in Portugal. What a country to visit. It's not like we were in each other's pockets, Hannes and I had our own place, there were a few places between us all. Someone would throw out what crew were doing, and we would meet up, have rooftop pool hangs, Portuguese tarts and short black coffees. Heaven! Then at night we would go off on an adventure to explore the city. Lisbon was beautiful, the tiles, the artworks, the buildings; it was a wonderful place, not to mention the fresh seafood, cheeses, deli meats and chicken! Nando's has got nothing on this place! The weather was perfect, we had an amazing crew and lots of laughs. Next stop was Lagos for some beach time. That place reminds me of Byron Bay, you start at the beach, head to a bar, do a full lap and end up at the same bar with all the same people by the end of the night. It's not that big and we met more Aussies than planned, but everyone was lovely and up for a good time.

One story really stood out and we'll forever refer to it as the Portuguese stitch-up. One afternoon, we all met up to go and explore an old castle at sunset. We walked up and strolled around, and it was great, we took a couple of candid shots with the backdrop of the city in the distance as the sun set. As we were heading back down the hill, Brad, Lucy and I thought we would run ahead to find somewhere to eat. There was a large group of us, so rather than try and fit at a few small tables, we thought it'd be smart to get to a big one first. There were a few good options, all the food we had eaten so far had been excellent. We popped our head into one place that caught our eye and asked the owner if he had room for 12.

'Of course!' he said excitedly.

'Come, sit down, I will give you a big table outside. It's perfect weather and I will give you a free bottle of port,' he continued.

He had us at free bottle of port. Hannes and I had done a walking tour that day and I had only just found out that port was made famous in Portugal.

Sure, thinking back, none of us particularly liked port, but it seemed like an offer too good to pass up; in hindsight, it was too good to be true.

We texted the others and flagged them down as they walked past. It was a pretty touristy area compared to the other places we had been dining at and was packed with crowds.

The waiter came over to our table, he was very on the ball.

'Hello, thank you for dining. Here is your free bottle of port to enjoy. Who wants a beer, who wants wine?'

We all raise our hands. Beers, bottles of wine, we wanted it all.

He tells us, rather than give us a menu, why doesn't he bring out some local smoked meats, cheeses, bread rolls, then for the main, two platters of fresh local seafood, and then two platters of meat with all the sides, with some rice, potatoes and vegetables.

We all nod and say yes, sounds perfect. It's like he was reading our minds. We were starving and he knew how to work the crowd.

The cheeses and meats came out, it was only enough for us all to have a slice of prosciutto each and one sliver of cheese. We devoured it so fast.

He came back and suggested another serve of the meat and cheese.

We said yes please, that was amazing.

Next was the seafood. I kid you not, these were two of the biggest platters of seafood I had ever seen. Fish fillets, whole fish, sardines, mussels, octopus, prawns, it was unbelievable, super tasty and so fresh. The platters were so big however, we couldn't possibly get through them, especially if there were meat ones to come. There was no physical way, and we were decent eaters. When more bottles of wine and beer came, we realised we'd have to cancel the meat platters. It was just too much food and no one was hungry, except one friend who'd been saving himself for the meat.

I ran inside to tell the man, we'd love them, but we need to cancel the meat platters, we are all too full. It is lovely food, but we just can't fit anymore in. I apologised.

He looks pissed off, but there was already so much food on the table, more would have just gone to waste.

We ask for the bill and it arrives.

It's 900 Euros.

We are in shock, but also laughing because it all makes sense now.

I tell the guys, feeling bad as we were the ones that picked the restaurant, that I will go and ask for an itemised bill as there must be some mistake.

By way of comparison, Hannes and I were out for lunch that day, had fresh seafood by the water as well as starters, salads and sides and six beers in total, and it was 25 Euros for the two of us. How could this be 900?

I look at the bill and my jaw drops. Turns out Mr Smooth Operator aka 'You don't need menus, we can organise the food for you' had ripped us off completely, charging us for the butter, the rolls – the platter of six slices of prosciutto alone cost 50 Euros. Thank fuck I cancelled the meat as the seafood is 200 Euros per platter. I ask him, is there a mistake, six slices of prosciutto is 50 Euros? He tells me it's no mistake, that's the price. I run back out to the group with my tail between my legs. We got stitched up hard core. I try to explain, everyone just starts laughing at the wild ride we were just on, knowing it was a touristy area, we didn't look at the menu, had no idea how much a beer even was and went hard on the recommendation from the owner. You've got to fucking laugh!

Brad yells out, 'Well, everyone drink up, because now we know why the port was free!'

We finish the port, split the bill, everyone was stuffed and had lots to drink. Our mates say, don't worry, if we were in Melbourne, we would happily pay $75 each for that spread and sure it was Euros so close to $100, but everyone just laughed. They said the food was good, the company was good, but we just must remember the time we got the ol' Portuguese stitch-up. That one has gone down in the books as the ultimate.

Portuguese stitch-up aside, the manymoon was a raging success. Hannes announced every year for our wedding anniversary we should all go away together because it was the best holiday with best friends and should become our new tradition. I knew he would come around.

MARRIED LIFE

The first thing that happens after you get married is people start asking you when you are having children. This question becomes standard conversation and to be perfectly honest it's really fucking annoying.

Do not get me wrong, I love kids and Hannes and I do want to have a family. We've discussed these things since the moment we got together. We have an honest relationship where communication is a huge part of it. I guess this is what happens when a relationship starts out long distance; you have to be good at talking openly with one another.

Another thing that I think people find difficult to understand is Hannes and I really enjoy our freedom. We like to go on holidays, nights out with mates, fancy dinners, have lazy Sundays that involve a sleep-in till noon if we feel so inclined; we enjoy it all. We both focus on work and staying healthy, but we also know how to have a good time together. Settling down comes in different phases for people and Hannes and I have enjoyed being married and not having kids just yet. I know the clock is ticking and it's important, as age does become a defining factor. The truth is, we haven't even tried. We know we would be good parents, but the timing hasn't been right.

The other huge elephant in the room is our family support network. Hannes' whole family live in Germany, we live in a different state to the rest of my family. We would be doing it completely alone. If I am going to become a mother, like everything in my life, I need to give 100 percent and be ready to commit to it.

My mum's health was also a huge factor. Living with terminal cancer, Mum's health was declining not improving. If I was pregnant or had a little baby, do you think I would be able to get on a plane to Sydney every few months, drop everything when I had to or even just to surprise Mum with a weekend trip? The answer to that is no! It wouldn't have worked, one income with a family and a sick mother.

My mum was my priority, she'd been my priority since I was 19 and found out my dad was having an affair. I wish I could shake this feeling and it isn't resentful at all, it's just being honest. If you had no family support network and a mother that god forbid might not be around for the next 12 months, could you do this? People have told me you just make it work, but I am guessing those people aren't in the same situation as me. They told me it would make Mum happy if I had a baby. When I spoke to Mum about this, as we had no secrets and it was a hot topic in our daily chats, Mum would tell me not to rush. I was fit, healthy and in love, and when it was the right time for us it would happen. Mum's words didn't sway my judgement, but they made me realise – and my mum would never have said this – she needed me more than I needed a baby.

That is a decision I made and have no regrets about. One day maybe I'll feel differently, but as long as I am honest with myself and my husband, I think that's all that really matters.

So married life didn't change us too much at all. We are still the same couple. I took my husband's family name; lucky he was cute, really. I did it because I think there is an old-fashioned respect in taking your partner's name once you get hitched.

ADVENTURES

My husband and I are lucky that we have had the opportunity to travel so much together. I was late when it came to being bitten by the travel bug, pretty much once I started dating a European. Going somewhere you have never been before and the chance you will never go there again excites us both. We love adventures together, they make us feel alive.

The last trip we did was to Vietnam, a stunning country. Beautiful people, food and a crazy history. We started in Ho Chi Minh City and ended up in Hanoi by travelling along the whole country. We travelled via plane, bus, sleeper train, boat, coach, private driver and bike. We really did it all.

Our favourite part of this holiday was when we went to a town called Sapa, in the mountains. We wanted to do a homestay with a private guide, and I had researched and found one that seemed suited to us. We wanted to learn about the culture, the area and the tribe we stayed with.

Our guide's name was Pang and she was an amazing woman. I feel blessed that I even got to spend time with her. She knows four languages which she taught herself, is married and has two young boys and such a knowledge of the area and its history. She was explaining wild things to us which were hard to comprehend. How in Sapa, near the border of China, every few days a girl is kidnapped. China has some pretty insane laws and some terrible decisions were made when it came to children and keeping the one child they could have as a boy; now there aren't enough women in the country for the men to marry, so they kidnap girls who are sold off and never seen again. It is well known in Sapa and the stories are heartbreaking. It happened to our tour guide's neighbour and her cousin. She also told us about the war, when the French invaded this area and turned Sapa into a French colony. Her tribe, the Black Hmong, almost got tricked into fighting against the Vietnamese for France and America, and then afterwards, didn't know where they sat as they were out on their own. War is a crazy, devastating time; it was so interesting to hear about all these hardships they had faced yet they were happy people.

Pang had such a lovely warm nature and opened her house to us and welcomed us into her family. We spent two days hiking through the landscape that was so diverse, from mountains, to rice paddy fields, to rivers, even through a bamboo forest. You could imagine a tiger bouncing out from behind the shadows. Pang informed us there were no tigers left, the people learnt to live off the land for food and now there aren't as many native animals as there had been. As she put it, they were eaten or killed during the war.

They didn't have much but her family was happy and healthy, her sons taught us how to prepare the vegetables for dinner while Pang taught us how to prepare the other food. They used everything and we all had to pull our weight, then after dinner was eaten and the dishes were done, we enjoyed 'happy water' as she called it, which was rice wine. It packed a punch! Six shots later it didn't even matter that you weren't sleeping on a plush mattress after walking 14 kilometres that day. A beautiful meal cooked over an open fire and then happy water to top it off, we were content, and as the name suggests, the water sure did make us happy. It really puts things in perspective when you have an experience like this. Pang had all she needed, she told us, a roof over her head, two healthy boys and a husband who not only loved her but was very strong.

Even in the mountains of Sapa my mum was on my mind. I couldn't shake the feeling something wasn't right. I had been in contact with Mum while I was away, updating her and my siblings in the family group chat about my travels and the adventures we had been on. That day however, I knew Mum was getting her latest scan results. It had been six months since her last scan, and I was nervous. I tried to call my family but no one got back to me. Finally before bed I thought I would try one more time to reach Mum.

'Hello, Chookie,' I said when I heard her say hello.

'Darling, you shouldn't have called. We can talk once you're back,' Mum replied.

'We can talk now, I have reception in the mountains and I wanted to check in and see how your day was.'

There is a pause, she seems flat.

I continue, 'You got your scan results today Mum, no one wrote in the chat and updated me and I have been waiting all day to hear the news. Are they not good?'

There is another pause.

'We can talk about it later,' Mum says, defeated.

'Not later, you know the rules, you can't keep it a secret from me! What's happened? It's not good otherwise someone would have written something. Has it spread? How bad is it?' I say, trying to hold back any emotion from my voice.

'Tunny, it has spread.'

'Okay, and like always, we will work through it. Where is it Mum, please tell me,' I am begging now.

'They found a spot at the base of my brain.'

She pauses.

'It's small but it's now moved there.'

I take a deep breath, in and out.

Now it's my time to pause.

I freeze and then realise I still haven't said anything.

'Right Mum, okay, thank you for telling me. It's no good me finding this out tomorrow or the next day or even when I am back home, do you understand Mum? The news and results are still the same and I know you like to protect us kids, but it doesn't help if we can't work through it together,' I say, choking on my tears.

'You're right, Darling,' Mum agrees.

I continue, 'Okay, so they have found it in this new spot. This isn't good news, and it's not what we expected, but like always Mum, we will work through it. I am sure they have already reached out about a treatment plan.'

'Yes, there is talk of surgery but it's risky in that area.'

I think about Mum's last biopsy and how even that small procedure took Mum a lot longer to recover from compared to the last time. Surgery wouldn't be an option.

Mum continues, 'I can start radiation on the area or I can do nothing.'

'Mum, I know we have said this before – it's your choice. Let's all have a think. Do you want to keep fighting?'

'Yes.'

'Okay, well let's discuss it with the kids and have a chat together as a family, we will support your choice and we will stand by you, whatever you decide. I love you, Mum, you know I do! Around the world and back again. I know you're stubborn, but thank you for telling me the truth.'

Mum laughs. She knows that she's more stubborn than me and that says a lot. We say our goodbyes and I tell her I will call her tomorrow.

I get off the phone and cry.

I cry while I am sitting in a bedroom, in a hut, at a homestay in the mountains of Sapa. I cry because that's all I can do. I am so devastated!

Her brain? Her brain, are you fucking kidding me? This is a whole new level of fucked. I didn't know much about brain cancer; even though it was still classed as breast cancer, it was now in the spinal fluid, that's how it travelled from her vertebrae to her brain, and from there it could go anywhere. The brain controls everything, her speech, her movement; the growth rate could be enormous. It was not fucking fair. It never was! I had prayed to god again and again. Please look after my mum, please keep her alive. I was just sitting on the bed in shock. When Hannes came into the room to check on me, he knew by the tears in my eyes and the look on my face the news wasn't good.

That night I closed my eyes and again thought of all the things I couldn't do to help save Mum. Between the tears and the exhaustion from the hike and the happy water I somehow managed to get to sleep. My dreams were vivid and wild like my emotions. I knew if I slept, tomorrow would be a new day and I just needed to get through the night and things would seem clearer in the morning.

The next day we said our farewells to Pang and thanked her for being a generous host. We assured her we'd recommend the trip and one day we hoped to be back. We ended our tour with the next stop which was Hanoi, we had a seven-hour coach ride ahead of us. I called Mum and checked in before we left. She sounded better, she had decided to give radiotherapy a go. The relief I felt was like I had been holding my breath. We might still have a chance, we might still buy some time. On the coach it was dark and I was listening to an extremely sad audiobook that was nearing the end. It is called *A Little Life*, and if you have read it, you will know what I am talking about. The book was traumatic, and it suited my mood because in the dark of the coach, I cried silent tears, for the book, for my mum, and I cried for myself.

LAST CHRISTMAS WITH MUM

I knew this Christmas with Mum was important, more special than usual. Although we didn't know it yet, it would be our very last Christmas with her.

It had become a new tradition for Mum and Dana to come to Melbourne and celebrate Aussie Christmas with us, and we loved it. As we always flew to Sydney for Serbian Orthodox Christmas on 7 January, we liked to play host on 25 December. As well as Mum and Dana, and Michael if he could make it, we had ring-ins and orphan friends who couldn't get home for Christmas. Everyone was welcome. I always prepared way too much food, we always had way too much booze and the baby pool was always filled up and ready for dipping.

This Christmas was different, Mum hadn't been well at all. She was generally not well, living with terminal cancer, but it had spread and she was far worse. By now it was in her vertebrae, liver, lungs and it was that October we'd found out it had gone to her brain.

The thing is, I had seen Mum in November. She had started a new session of radiotherapy for the third time in her life. She was rocking a great new wig, red this time. Mum liked to change it up. I'd taken her out for the day for a drive and some lunch. Mum seemed good, she had an energy and positive vibe about her. She was determined this time she would beat it.

A few days before Christmas Eve when she and Dana arrived, Hannes called me to come help get the girls out of the car. I was busy in the kitchen preparing a cheese board and a mezze grazing platter, my signature move for when any guests arrived.

When I got outside, I ran to give Mum the biggest hug. As I was approaching the car, I noticed Mum didn't have a wig on, instead rocking her short hair that had just started growing back a few weeks prior from her last round of chemo. I also noticed Mum was using her walking stick again, but this time really needed it, and not only the walking stick, but another person beside her for support.

It then hit me like a slap in the face – this would be our last Christmas together. Even as I write this, the thought of it makes me tear up, reliving this heartbreaking realisation. As soon as I embraced Mum she started crying from happiness and I guess in hindsight sadness. I gave her a big cuddle as I always did and also put on a brave face and held back any tears. I had a rule, and that was not to cry in front of Mum. Once we got back into the house, I went to the bedroom just to take a few deep breaths. Hannes followed me in and asked if I was okay. I told him not to ask me again because I clearly wasn't and if he did ask me again, I would start crying and might not stop.

It was always amazing to have my mum come stay. I know she loved to brag about her trips to Melbourne where she stayed with her daughter and son-in-law. Dana loved a getaway just as much as Mum. Without exchanging words, I knew Dana knew as well that deep down this could be our last Christmas together and every moment counted.

Mum and I had a relationship where I called the shots. She didn't baby me like with my sister. Somehow over the years, especially since the affair, I tended to protect Mum. I just wanted to make sure she was always as comfortable as she could be, and anything I could do to help her, I would do in a flash. Once, Mum went to a clairvoyant who told her that in a past life she felt that I was her great-great-grandmother and was always protecting her, so maybe it's because of that and over the hundreds of years I have been programmed that way, or maybe it's just because she's my mum and I love her more than anything.

I'd bought a new lamp so she could read at night. She loved her books, just like me. I got a non-slip mat for the bathroom, so she wouldn't slip going in and out of the shower, and we also had to keep a stool in there for her balance. I got all her favourite food and sent her draft menus of what I had been planning for the Christmas feast and if she had any requests.

Mum would just say, 'Sounds wonderful, Tunny. Can't wait to see you both.'

I had a few days planned of activities, but due to Mum's health, most involved a lot of relaxing, eating and drinking. It was Christmas after all. I tried to think of things within walking distance, so even with Mum's legs not working as well, she could still enjoy her holiday in Melbourne as planned. We went to the movies and to the markets where Mum enjoyed a coffee and relaxed while Dana and I ran around to get our Christmas supplies. We took the girls to the pub for a parma and a beer and sat in the sun, one of our favourite Melbourne traditions.

One night, we ate at a local fancy restaurant. Mum is so funny and embarrassing like all parents. I told her quietly that the man walking around was the owner and lived in our street. I'd never actually met the bloke before, I just knew as we had seen him around. Of course Mum, who loves chatting just as much as I do, asked him, 'So you live locally, do you?'

He answered Mum in his thick Italian accent.

'Yes!' He confirmed he was the owner and did live on our street.

After that he kept coming over to chat to us all, he sent out his nephew, his staff, everyone wanted to talk to us. At the end of the meal he asked if we would like dessert on the house. How could we say no! At the time I was like ah, cringe Mum, you had to, didn't you, but now I love it as when we walk past they always wave or ask us to come in for a coffee on the house.

Christmas Eve, we had friends over for dinner to join us. The more the merrier is my theme for the festive season. We had turkey, cranberry sauce, vegan-coated cauliflower topped with a red sauce and pistachios, fresh green salads and oven-roasted vegetables. I had even made a golden gaytime trifle which was such a hit a few Christmases ago, I made it again as the perfect end to the feast.

Before dinner, Mum came to relax with us and enjoy a champagne downstairs in the courtyard, which I had decked out in a classic red-themed festive setting. She had a big beaming smile on her face that said without words I had done an amazing job once again.

Even though Mum tried so hard to enjoy the evening, it was

obvious she was in a lot more pain than usual. She was putting on a brave face, but she had to have her dinner in bed. She loved to socialise, but she couldn't do it, she was uncomfortable and exhausted. I brought up the food to her and made sure she was cosy in bed; she said she enjoyed it just as much and was so pleased to see my lovely friends again.

Christmas Day, same deal again. Food galore! We had cold leg Christmas ham – in theory you could have leg ham any time of year, but it is a special treat to share with your loved ones and this has always been an important part of what makes Christmas to us, running to the fridge for a sliver of cold ham! Heaven! I also had the rest of the classics, snapper on the BBQ, oysters, prawns, plenty of salads (one being ajvar, which is oven-roasted capsicum pickled with oil, garlic, pepper and chilli – Baba used to have an unlimited supply in her fridge and we'd have a dollop of it with a slice of cheese on her fresh homemade bread) as well as my famous mac and cheese, and to top it off, traditional Christmas pudding with custard and ice-cream for dessert. I put a chair in the baby pool so Mum could dip her legs in. It was a perfect summer's day, and just like me this woman loved the sun. It's a family trait. We were feasting, pumping the Christmas tunes, all the '60s and '70s favourites were our family jams. Christmas was a success, we were all wiped out from over-eating, over-drinking, over-talking and pretty much over-indulging.

The day before they flew out, we took the girls to the beach. Mum loves the ocean, something about that sea air always feels healing and cleansing to the soul. Mum needed a helping hand to walk on the sand, and we set up a chair. She told me she wanted to feel the water.

Now, as I reflect on this moment, I see it as a very special memory, one that will stay with me forever. At the time I didn't realise, but it would be the last time in her life Mum would ever feel the ocean on her tired legs. This would be the last time we would ever spend at the beach, Mum with her girls, the last time sand would get everywhere it wasn't meant to be, the last time Mum would catch and throw the ball to us, the last time I would see her at her happy place.

Our Serbian Christmas, the whole shebang again, was in Manly. We drove up this time, and had a few catch-ups planned with friends, lunch dates and dips at the beach, as well as Christmas celebrations. It was our summer holiday after all.

For Christmas Day, we go all-out – full table setting, candles, freshly baked bread, the delicious Christmas spread. As we celebrate with my Kuma and her family, there ends up being about 20 of us. We were lucky Kuma was also Mum's next door neighbour. Mum was visibly worse, in a lot more pain, a lot more tired and fatigued. We noticed this as soon as we arrived, and we had only seen her a few days prior in Melbourne. Rather than the walking stick, Mum was now using a walker to walk even a short distance of three metres. She had her next MRI booked in for 9 January, so we were anxious about what the results would be. In the meantime, it was all systems go for key family time, us kids were giving Mum our all.

Mum and Kuma lived in an over-55s apartment block. Kuma's family and us kids laugh our heads off at the stories we hear about that place. You could write a comedy skit about all the interesting characters who live there. One example is Glenda, who is 100 years old and a kleptomaniac. She steals people's belongings from outside their apartments and will just start wearing or using them as her own. She has no shame or remorse because, well, she's 100. I guess her attitude is, 'Fuck you all, I will do what I want.' Once she stole Mum's chair from her balcony. Kuma, being someone who puts up with absolutely zero bullshit, called her out on it. They saw her walking away with it, so they approached her and asked for it back. She was pulling the chair along, determined to take off with it; picture it, a hundred-year-old woman, getting caught in the act of stealing a chair, and still not giving it up. I mean the balls on this woman! After Kuma managed to grab the chair just as the lift doors were closing, Glenda pointed her walking stick at them both and said, 'Well, you're too fat and you're too thin!' Mum had the chair back in her arms again and that was the end of that.

We were setting up the table in the communal space on the top floor, which has an incredible view right around to Circular Quay. Since Mum moved in, we'd been holding our Christmases here as her studio apartment was a bit tiny for all of us.

In strolls Glenda, wearing Mum's friend's sneakers that she stole from her front door. We know this as Pat was helping us set up the table and mentioned it in passing. Now here's Glenda, who waltzes in, sits down and puts her feet up, in Pat's shoes, on the coffee table, and stares at us.

Kuma tells her off in English and then in Serbian. Mum then asks in a softer tone, 'Glenda, you can't put your feet up on the table, Darling, because people eat off there, it's unhygienic.'

Glenda looks through Mum and chooses to ignore her, then out of the blue, a volunteer that helps people out around the apartments pipes up.

'Can you take your feet down, it's not a good idea. People eat off that table,' she politely asks.

Glenda then takes her feet down and smiles sweetly.

Once the volunteer leaves the room, Glenda gets out her middle finger and flips Mum the bird! Fucking Glenda. Gives zero fucks, 100 years old and gives people the bird! My brother laughed, 'You can't help but admire her attitude!' which you've got to agree is just outstanding!

We all enjoyed another excellent Serbian Christmas as a family. Mum could pop to her room and rest when she needed to, she never once complained, she didn't whinge about the pain and the situation. Mum was always so positive! She was just so thankful and so happy to have her beautiful children around her. That night in true Christmas style, whoever was still up would kick on drinking many more bottles of wine. It was Christmas round two after all.

The next day, however, things weren't good. Mum woke up in more pain, you could see it on her face, she was wincing. Mum's pain threshold is extremely high. Once she broke her arm slipping down a steep wet driveway and landed hard on her elbow. She didn't go to the doctor for at least five days, but then her arm turned black and blue. She had shattered her elbow.

When I saw this look on Mum, I panicked, but it's my job to stay cool and calm. No tears! Us kids took Mum to Emergency. We waited around, and they went through the usual questions. See, the trouble is when they asked Mum what was wrong, it was not as simple as pointing and saying, 'I have pain here.'

Mum was describing how she felt.

'My legs feel like fire and ice, it's a numb sensation, like walking on ice blocks.'

Mum explains her legs had been getting worse and worse. Her last lot of radio was on the brain in November, and her chemo in October. The big problem was, everyone was targeting Mum's brain tumour, so she hadn't been on any other treatment, other than direct radio on the brain which was so confronting to watch. To do it, they made a special mould of her face and Mum got screwed into this mask, so she could not move even a quarter of a millimetre. Then the whole bed she'd be lying on would slide into a big machine where she'd receive the radiotherapy. As all this had been going on, there was no other treatment to any other part of her body, so the liver and lungs had been neglected. The focus was the brain. Our main concern was that the tumour had got worse and was affecting her balance and movement. Would it affect her speech or more of her motor skills next?

So Mum was explaining for the hundredth time what was wrong – the pain in her legs that radiates up her body around her spine, at about nine out of 10, and this is a scale that doctors use for pain where 10 is child birth! Mum was constantly sitting at nine on a good day.

We spent hours at the hospital that day, and to make matters worse, the doctor on duty was a real fucking bitch. While explaining what was going on with her legs, Mum also loved to bring up her Baker's cysts, which caused us kids to roll our eyes with a smirk; we knew this was not what was affecting her balance, but Mum being Mum loved to explain, 'They are quite painful, you know.' She couldn't walk. Something more serious was happening and it was connected to the cancer somehow. Mum was meant to have her MRI the next day. We asked if she could have it today seeing as though we were here and there was obviously something very wrong.

Doctor Dickhead was rude to Mum, she couldn't understand why she was asking to reschedule an MRI. The doctor didn't want to consider Mum's cancer history but wanted to treat her as a new case.

The point was, Mum's legs worked in late November and by early January had almost stopped completely.

After sitting around for five hours, we got Mum something to eat, the poor thing hadn't even had breakfast, we were in such a rush to get her to hospital. We decided on one of her favourites, a Big Mac! Come on, what's not to love? The bun, meat, pickles, special sauce, boom! It makes me laugh thinking about it. Doctor Dickhead still hadn't even done one blood test. Mum was so hungry that as the doctor was talking to her, Mum was eating the burger in such a hurry, as the poor woman was starving. At the same time, the nurse didn't know how to work the bed and it was somehow closing Mum in half as she was scoffing down the burger. At one stage Mum's legs were in the air and it almost looked like she was giving birth, all while chowing down on some Maccy D's! The vision was 10/10, Mum giving zero fucks to this doctor! The doctor even commented that if Mum stayed, she might not make her MRI tomorrow. This was Mum's first scan in months, it was crucial. We all knew that if Mum was making her MRI, we needed to get her the fuck out of that hospital, so we discharged her and went home.

The next day we took it really easy, we just let Mum rest and kept an eye on her. We managed to get her to her MRI and were scheduled to meet with her radiologist the following day for the results. My brother and I were meant to be leaving Sydney by now, but as we had a feeling something more sinister was going on, we decided to postpone our trips home.

The radiologist seemed professional and caring. Mum described him as having big brown eyes and a beautiful smile which was true; he seemed to have caring eyes. We sat down for the results together preparing for the worst, but hoping for the best. I was unaware that this line would become my mantra. He explained to us there was too much swelling on the brain to see if the radio had worked. This was not the news we'd been hoping for. As well as all the Endone, Targin and Panadol Mum had been on, she'd also been on steroids to help with this swelling, so in theory, they were meant to help with her movement, appetite and motor skills; at the same time, they'd eat away at her muscle and body strength almost causing her strength to wither away. Like every fucking thing cancer-related you take the bad side effects to help ease even worse issues from the actual disease, but it's always a catch-22. The doctor continued explaining the results, which were also not what we'd hoped for – they found new spots that had popped up in the short window since radio started.

He was also concerned about this new pain in her legs and the issue with her mobility, even though there was a chance they were caused by leptomeningeal disease, which it was looking like Mum most likely had. He decided to keep her in hospital and booked her in for an MRI from the lungs down.

You might be thinking, why didn't they do that already? Or the day before, why didn't Doctor Dickhead scan her whole body? Or weeks prior when Mum had been complaining of excruciating pain? Truth be told, they are meant to be the professionals, but fuck me, if I had a dollar for every goddamn time we'd felt neglected by people in the medical world, people not taking her pain and symptoms seriously enough, I'd be bloody rich. Mum's results came in fast the next day, we were all there, and we were all prepared for the news.

Mum's breast cancer, which had already been metastatic, had travelled again and this time developed in her lower back and spine. Mum didn't just have one new growth, but multiple tumours, one already as big as a golf ball.

Even though Mum had been doing every goddamn thing right, it didn't matter; it had spread again and this time was affecting her mobility. Her radiologist had arranged for Mum to start radio on this area ASAP where she would get blasted with five sessions over the next seven days. Mum had only just had radio a few months prior on the brain, but this was the plan of attack; it was our best option out of all the terrible options that lay before us.

My brother and I asked to speak to the radiologist alone. We told Mum and Dana we would catch up with them. We tried to make it sound casual, but the reality was we had some important direct questions to ask and we needed some honest answers privately. We asked him point-blank what is his diagnosis on our mother?

He looked at us with those big brown eyes full of sadness and told us that our darling mother only had a few months left to live.

This news. Here it was. For almost six years, we knew at some stage a doctor would tell us these exact words. I knew it would come, but I always told myself how thankful I was that we had never had that conversation before, that as bad as it had been, the doctors and her team were always thinking about the next step or the next hurdle. So even if I had these thoughts, I had somehow pushed them all the way to the very bottom of my mind; they came on when I went for a run or late at night when I was trying to sleep or even enjoying a moment listening to a song I loved. But when the radiologist told us, I had to take really deep breaths to hold back my emotions to continue to hear what this professional had to say.

He explained they were looking at her month by month now, not in blocks of a year or even six months. Every week mattered now. Our job would be to keep her quality of life as high as it could be, for what would be the final stages of her life. He started using words like 'time limit', 'palliative care', 'respite', 'rehab' and 'terminal'. Words that I had heard before and knew full well what they meant, but for the first time in my life, I knew their true meaning and it sent sharp pain directly to my heart. You hear about moments in time where you can feel your heart actually breaking – I was there. This news sent wet stinging salty tears to my eyes. We thanked him for being honest, he handed us his business card and told us to contact him directly if we had more questions.

Michael suggested we go to the bathroom before we see the girls and digest what just happened, cry for a bit. I hadn't seen my young adult brother cry since my grandmother's funeral some five years ago. We hugged and cried and hugged and cried some more. It doesn't matter if you know someone with a terminal disease or not, even if we had a slight inkling it was coming, even if Mum was the healthiest woman in the world. To be told such news about anyone in this world you care about, it hits you so hard. It's a shocking realisation as the thing you have dreaded the most suddenly comes true; that feeling is gut-wrenching and heartbreaking and makes you feel a sadness you haven't ever felt before.

My brother and I made a pact then and there that we cannot mourn our mother while she is alive. We need to keep positive and keep supporting each other with the energy we have and tackle this like we have every other time, with our heads held high, and that's what we tried to do. Although that night was hard, I was drained, we all were. We felt like we had been holding our breath, and suddenly the air escaped and we had nothing, nothing left to give. I cried in the shower and then cried myself to sleep. Holding in emotion like that is hard, being strong is even harder, but sometimes when it leaks out, through a sob, a tear or a tremble in your voice, it's hard to keep it locked away. Once it starts, it's hard to stop. Tomorrow would be a new day.

Mum stayed in hospital over the course of her latest instalments of radiotherapy – seven days. The plan for after her treatment still hadn't been decided, but for now we were playing it day by day pending how she reacted, how her pain management was and how her legs were. I extended my stay in Sydney so I could be with her. I spent every day by her side at the hospital, I would bring her a coffee every day on my way in and we would have morning tea together. I was trying to juggle working remotely, spending time with Mum and making sure she was comfortable and eating.

This was a strange time in my life between my actual life at home, my husband, friends and job in Melbourne. The desire and need to be in Sydney with Mum were strong; even if there wasn't anything I could physically do, being there helped calm me and it felt as though it made a difference somehow. Mum was still working towards getting back to independent living, but this goal kept slipping further and further away.

I take my hat off to families going through this hardship because it absolutely shatters your world and you forget how normal feels. From social workers to My Aged Care to MyGov, not to mention all the doctors and specialists giving you different information, it's information overload. You feel helpless and that no one understands your situation and that you might not know how to deal with things. They expect you to know and it's so frustrating. Your emotions are high and communication lacks between all parties. I would come back from spending the day at the hospital drained and emotional.

One night I thought I'd clean Mum's fridge out. There were vegetables and food in her crisper that had gone bad and needed to be thrown out. That night I cried myself to sleep, tears running down my face stinging my eyes. It hit me that night that Mum needed full-time care – if she couldn't reach the bottom drawer of her fridge anymore, it was obvious she couldn't live at home on her own. If Mum couldn't bend, she also wouldn't be able to get up if she had a fall. This was a devastating realisation as I knew her apartment in Manly was something she was so proud of. Her cancer had never stopped her living a normal life to an extent, but suddenly that was changing, and so rapidly.

After many conversations and much research, Mum moved into a respite facility that offered beds for a limited window of time for someone to have respite from a sick family member or for a family member that is between two types of care. In your mind you think they are different places, but respite facility is just another name for a nursing home. Mum's options were to go home with two hours' support a fortnight with My Aged Care or palliative care full time, which her medical team didn't think she was ready for. The final option was respite where you could stay for up to nine weeks per calendar year. It seemed a better option and we were rushing into locking down anything.

Finding a suitable nursing home for my very trendy 67-year-old mother was maybe the worst job in the world. Mum had managed to get her hair cut and eyebrows done when she was in hospital. She had somehow convinced a nurse to take her to the salon downstairs. This is how much appearance mattered to her but not in a vain way, more because she took pride in how she looked. Mum was the only lady in the cancer ward I saw wearing red lipstick with matching nail polish.

There seems to be a gap in the market. I saw about nine on the Northern Beaches and not one was suitable. Mum had been assessed by ACAT as high risk, which meant most places offered her a shared bedroom and bathroom with a 90-year-old resident with dementia. I love old people, please don't get me wrong, but rewind to four weeks prior and Mum had been in her own place, still doing it all and this would have been a shock to anyone; it just made a shitty situation so much worse. What if you were 40 and this had happened to you or your daughter, there aren't any options and it's sad to know there is a huge gap in the system.

As I drove around, set up appointments and called nursing homes, it was shocking some of the reactions I got. Some were very caring and would tell me point-blank I had a terrible job to do, they were honest and fair and explained their options wouldn't be suitable for Mum. On the other hand, others were rude, short with me, looked at me like why was I there. I lost it with one lady, explaining to her Mum is 67 and dying from breast cancer, I live in another state and even if I was to relocate Mum to Melbourne, we had stairs which she could not use. She also had her friends, family and doctors in Sydney. I explained I had never had to deal with anyone going through this, but here I am trying to find my feet. Hoping and wishing I can find something that met enough of my mum's needs and values so she can feel comfortable and safe in her new home. Give me a fucking break and have some heart because you wouldn't wish this upon your worst enemy. I was trying my goddamn best.

I finally found one which was suitable for the time being. It had a nice view and a balcony and Mum would have her own bathroom. At this time Mum still thought she was going home, so we had a few arguments where I reasoned with her that if her pain calms down and her legs start working, we can get her home, we will do what it takes. Mum was still showering on her own, reading, socialising, the only difference being her location. Then Mum got an infection, and everything went rapidly downhill again.

Mum started to get confused, started saying some strange things. I'd call the head nurse for advice about what we should do as I had been back in Melbourne for five days, and Mum was not acting like herself. We were concerned. Sure, we knew it could be the brain tumour, but it could also be something else. After a few days of us being extremely concerned, a family friend who'd visited Mum suggested she could have a UTI. She told us that with all the drugs Mum was on, if she can't process them, they could be making her extremely foggy in the head. I called the palliative community care number that Mum was linked to and explained what I had been told. They called the head nurse and organised a test to be run on Mum. Turned out she did have a UTI, but this was at 7pm on a Friday. No doctors could see her to write her a prescription, so even though we knew what it was, no drugs to fix it could be supplied. Talk about another huge gap in the system!

This is what I didn't understand, she was at a high-care respite facility. They only ran the test because I called and spoke to someone that was using their brain, and no one could get my mum a script or a doctor to see her. It was insane. My attitude was, just sort it out and give Mum what she needs.

The options were to take Mum to Emergency, but it was so late by now and she was too unwell to wait around, and also, she was seeing things which was unsettling. Or our other option was to wait till the next morning when someone would come to see her and all would be sorted. Saturday morning came, no one came to see Mum. I think that morning my sister and I called every 24-hour hotline for doctors in the whole of Sydney. Turns out no one was working that day in that area. I called Dana in a panic after getting advice from a registered nurse on one of the hotlines – not the registered nurse at Mum's facility. She informed me if it had been a few days, we needed to get Mum to hospital now, call an ambulance and get her seen. She said it with such urgency that I knew it was serious.

Mum ended up back in hospital, this time for two days. She had a severe UTI and had started to turn a shade of yellow while she got further testing done. On the Sunday, the day after Mum had arrived, the head of oncology spoke to my sister. She explained that in addition to the UTI, Mum's liver was starting to fail. My sister called me in tears, I was already in tears before the call even came, I had a feeling and it was not a good one. I had been worried sick, and I was in Melbourne and felt so far away. That morning Hannes and I had gone to the beach early, down Mornington way. We'd taken our paddleboards out and gone exploring around the Bay. We were laughing and I was teasing him about something like I always do. I had no idea that this was the last day I would have a normal morning with my husband for a very long time.

It was decided that Mum was now ready for palliative care and would be transferred to a palliative care hospital the very next day. I booked flights and arrived by Monday. Palliative care sounded scary as from what I knew about it, which really wasn't much at all, it was where people went to die.

Mum was surrounded by love. There was a presence that you could feel when you entered the room she was in. She had this sunshine about her, it radiated all around her. When I walked into her room, I realised Mum was exactly where she needed to be.

Her room had been set up by Dana and Nada, Mum's sister from another mister, with little touches that made it welcome. She had a tea set, she had a bar trolley, she had her clothing and books. The next day I added my little touches, her salt lamp, her dreamcatcher and her speakers. Mum also had a custom-made leopard-print wheelchair which Nada had decked out for her.

We wanted to create an environment that surrounded Mum in love. It's what she deserved.

We wanted her to feel cherished by her kids, the way she always made us feel. Safe, secure and with music always playing – this was a must. My brother had flown in from interstate so Mum's three kids were there. It didn't matter what was happening in the world, we were where we needed to be.

The doctors and team working there were incredible. Finally it felt like Mum was getting the attention she'd needed this whole time. The doctors would spend up to an hour a day talking to Mum as well as pulling us kids aside privately and keeping us well informed. We learnt a lot in a short time frame, and the respect I have for the people that dedicate their lives to working there is endless. There are volunteers that come through with, I kid you not, a booze trolley known as the Jolly Trolley. They knock or pop their head in and ask, 'Who needs a drink?' And if you have a loved one lying in bed in this place, let me tell you, you need a fucking drink.

We took turns spending the night with Mum. The staff organised a futon for the room. We could at least lie down and trick our mind into thinking, well, I might not be sleeping, but I have my eyes closed and I am horizontal, so this might be as good as it gets for the evening, and trust me, it helps. The UTI was finally starting to clear so Mum was getting sharper each day. This also doubled as a bit of false hope. We thought, wow, maybe Mum is getting better? She seems more with it. The doctor explained due to Mum's liver starting to shut down, she would get a bit more yellow, a bit more off her food, a bit more swollen and a bit more tired every day until one day she didn't wake up. But we'd feel hopeful because some days we would see more of Mum shining through, she had more of a gleam in her eyes and more colour in her face, making cheeky remarks, but then she would see things as well. She kept seeing babies everywhere in the room, she kept feeling the presence of children. She also thought she was pregnant. As her jaundice got worse, the swelling in her feet and ankles and her stomach was getting worse. We still aren't sure where her feeling of being pregnant came from. She would whisper it like it was a secret.

'Tania, Darling, I need to tell you something and I don't know how to do it. I am expecting a baby!'

'Mum, I don't think that is possible.'

'I know, but I am.'

'But Mum, you haven't been having sex.'

Holding back laughter now, I'd add that she'd also had a hysterectomy many years ago.

Then, with a really concerned look on her face, Mum would say, 'Shit, you are right, I have! That is so weird,' she would agree.

Then we would talk about something else and a few days later it would circle back again to the baby she was having.

Staying over seemed strange in theory. Never did I think I would spend that much time at a hospital, eating when we remembered to, having a shower there when I stayed the night, but it was our new normal and we all just accepted it. Our focus was Mum, and her wellbeing became all that mattered. Who needs eight hours' sleep, getting a workout in, eating three meals a day, none of that shit mattered. Sure, in the real world it absolutely did, but in this bubble that had become our life nothing else mattered but Mum.

Behind the scenes Michael and I had started to clear Mum's apartment when we weren't on the night shift. We had a Salvation

Army pile, as well as a pile for us kids. This seemed like a fucking bizarre thing to do. My husband was struggling to understand how we could do it, but the reality was we had to. No one else would and it gave us a purpose when we weren't with Mum. We had a to-do list and we were on autopilot.

The shit part was Mum didn't know or chose not to believe she was never coming home. We never could chat to her about it as she still always said she was coming home. In our conversations, she would say something so adorable it would melt my heart, like, 'Aw, Tunny, you are so cute,' holding my hand as she said it.

She would also tell you that the chicken was back and was sitting in the tree outside, but now it was in the room crossing from one side to another and then in the same breath she would explain that once they worked out what was wrong with her, she would be home.

In hindsight, I wish we got to talk to Mum about her leaving this world behind. We tried, we really did, but she just didn't want to accept it. I get it though, to admit that to your kids, as a mum it would be so hard. She was our rock, she had always been the one stable part of our life. She was always the same and we could rely on her to be there. Mum was always so brave, she fought breast cancer as though it was a bad fall off a bike. She would, every damn time, just get back up and dust herself off, put on a new helmet (in her case, a new hairstyle or wig) and keep on riding because she didn't want to admit defeat and I admire her so much for this courage that poured through her soul.

As well as packing down her studio apartment, we also had to plan her funeral and we never got to ask her what she wanted because she refused to believe she was dying. The blind leading the blind, but we were hoping for the best and preparing for the worst. We had to honour Mum's Serbian Orthodox heritage and tradition, but with a modern touch, from wake venues to flowers to memorial cards to a casket. It's surreal and you can't actually comprehend what you're doing, but you do it because you have to.

During Mum's stay in palliative care, we had music playing all the time. Music was a big part of all our lives and Mum, the

Original Disco Chook, loved her jams from the '60s and '70s, and us kids did too.

We planned parties and dressed Mum up in the tutu skirt she had made for a reunion party she'd once attended, we went out and got fresh food, breads, cheeses, crackers, stuffed olives, marinated vegetables, meats from Italy and Spain, we brought the party to Mum.

We invited her brothers and a few times we managed to get her outside in the fresh air in her leopard-print wheels, but as she got more tired we would have our parties in the room and Michael would do a bit of rearranging to fit everyone in around the hospital bed. Someone would always be near her holding her hand. She was the guest of honour at a constant party, there was always someone who wanted to come and visit. I was slow-cooking meals overnight so we could enjoy family dinners together.

One day I tried to talk to Mum about what was on her list. As mentioned, Mum didn't accept things were coming to an end. I asked her, 'If you could have anything in the world, what would it be?'

Mum being Mum said she would like her toenails painted red, she'd love some mango gelato, and she asked me to text her friends, a married couple that she had known her whole life and tell them that she loved them and not to be sad. Finally, she asked if I could make her a Fluffy Duck which is her favourite cocktail. I said I could do all those things. The only thing she asked for that I couldn't do, which broke my heart, was take her to the beach, even if she just sat in her wheelchair to watch us throw the footy around. I told her we'd bring the ball to her room and see if we could have a play. We didn't want to diminish her hopes, as sometimes hopes and dreams are all we have.

By the next day I had done all on her to-do list except the beach trip, but the ball was now in her room. We were all sitting around listening to 'Brown Eyed Girl' by Van Morrison and 'Spirit in the Sky' by Norman Greenbaum, drinking our Fluffy Ducks, which are delicious. Bring back the Fluffy Duck!

Fluffy Duck
15 ml Cointreau
30 ml Advocaat
30 ml orange juice
30 ml white rum
30 ml cream
250 ml lemonade

Put ice cubes into the bottom of a cocktail glass.
Pour the spirits, then cream and orange juice on
the ice, then top with lemonade.

We did a lot of reflecting, on all the stories from our past, all the good times we had and all the laughs as well as the harder times. We reminisced and it felt good. I hadn't spent this much time with Mum and my siblings for a very long time, since I was a child really.

We became like the nursing staff, Mum's full-time carers. We would dress her, help her to the bathroom, and with brushing her teeth and feeding her. Feeding Mum was my brother's forte as he had an excellent way of making her eat as much food as possible. He was also patient and kind.

'What is this we have today, ooh, yum!'

'What's that Michael? Looks good!'

'Well Mum, seems to me that you have some deep sea mackerel, how good is that? If you don't mind, I might sample it just in case you don't want it,' he would smirk in reply.

'No, I would love some, sounds tasty, I think I ordered that.' Mum would take the bait every time.

The halls of that place became our hang-out. Every day you went in and time was irrelevant; all that mattered was that you were there.

One Saturday when we were having a party for Mum, again with a spread of her and our favourite mezze, Mum's doctor pulled us aside and asked to speak to us all privately. He explained Mum had a chest infection. She had only just beaten the UTI and now there was another one, this time in her chest, because Mum was getting weaker and weaker every day. The cancer just attacks when the immune system is down. This infection would be her last. He explained that Mum could try and have the antibiotics even though she had only just finished a course, but as her body was weaker, they may not work. We asked him what the benefits were, and he said it could buy Mum a few more days. We decided it was Mum's call to make, and he agreed to come back after our party to have the conversation with her while we were all by her side. Before the doctor came to speak to Mum, we wanted to talk to her about where she thought she was, where she would be going next, whether she knew why we were all there. Michael tried to be as diplomatic as possible. He sounded so calm and caring, and he got to the point, in a gentle way.

'Mum, you know where you are don't you?'

Mum nodded. 'I am at palliative care.'

'Mum,' he said so gently, 'the cancer is winning. I don't normally say the C word, it's a bit Voldemort for us, but Mum, you won't be leaving here, you're dying.'

Mum stares at him and says, 'But once I get my legs working in a few weeks, I will be fine.'

Dana, Mike and I were all holding her hands and looking at her so intensely. I could not look at Dana's or Mike's eyes. One glance I knew would set me off. I was trying to slow my breathing down, to keep control of my emotions, but I started to cry as it was all a little too real. Mum looked at me and asked me why I was crying. I explained that I was crying because I was sad. I asked her if she felt sad too and she said she did. She told us she felt safe, secure and well looked after, but she was sad and didn't know why. I knew why, I knew why I was sad and tearful, and I also knew exactly why she felt sad too, but for me to get those words out was impossible. I couldn't tell her, 'Mum, you are dying, we are heartbroken and we love you so goddamn much and we would be so upset if you left us, but we understand you're tired and need to let go, your body is exhausted and can't keep going, your liver isn't working…' I couldn't do anything but try to muffle my cries while I gave her little hand a kiss.

We left the room as we needed a timeout, and Mum practically kicked us out as her friend had come, all dressed up in a leopard-print trench coat, hat, top, gloves and sunnies, to perform a dance for her. My brother said while we were leaving the room, 'Well, that went absolutely nothing like I'd planned. Would've got more of a response from a brick wall.'

We all laughed. Fuck, it was classic Olga. In the face of death and danger, she looks at me and says why are you crying when she goddamn knows why I am. That night I called my husband and told him that my mum is the world's most stubborn woman apart from me, and good luck to him with me for the rest of his life. He just laughed because he knew no truer words had been spoken.

Once we returned to the room, the doctor was ready. He came in and greeted Mum in his quirky manner and sat down to ask her if they could have a talk. Mum nodded. He told her she had an infection and while they could give her antibiotics and they might work, there is a good chance they won't. Mum's body needed to be strong enough to fight. With the antibiotics, plus her liver failure, every tablet she took would weaken her.

He told Mum she was a smart wonderful woman. The first time he met her, she had a flower behind her ear. She took great care of herself and wore lovely red lipstick. He respected her decision to keep fighting and give the antibiotics a go.

Mum thanked him and said she couldn't remember the last time she'd looked in a mirror. We all reassured her she looked as glam as always. Mum and I had been doing a few sneaky face masks and I had been her go-to for night cleansing and moisturising as well as a full-body moisturising routine. As her poor swollen skin was so dry, we massaged Mum's skin with lotion. It seemed to help; even if it was a placebo effect, it made her feel better.

But then Mum's doctor got serious.

'Olga, I respect you as a woman, so now you must respect me as a doctor. We will start the course of antibiotics tonight, but the rules are as follows: You must be well enough to swallow the tablets on your own. We will not be doing tests on you further, and you need to understand there will be no more scans. You are too unwell to take to the hospital and I simply won't put you through it. My job is to make you comfortable, do you understand?'

Mum nodded again. 'Deal,' she said, and shook his hand.

He also asked if Mum had any unfinished business, whether there were any babies on the way? Not again. Mike and I, the ones in relationships, had been getting this line a lot in the last few weeks. He also mentioned in a very serious tone that there could be a movie or show that Mum really wanted to watch that could be her unfinished business. He said he once had a man that wanted to finish watching *Game of Thrones*, but got up to the last season and realised the show was not for him anymore. My brother and I are holding back laughter – if you have watched the last season of *GOT*, you know full well it is not worth holding on for. Mum however was unaware who Jon Snow was, so it was a blessing for her in this instance. If you know, you know!

Sunday came around and Mum had started sleeping more. We could only get her for a few hours a day when she was awake and involved in what was happening around her. We continued to listen to music and chat as though Mum was involved in all our conversations.

By the time Monday came around, there was a shift in Mum's mood and presence. She was sleeping a lot longer and wasn't eating. Not even Michael, the snack master himself, could make Mum eat more than a couple of teaspoons full. We all had a terrible feeling that what we had been preparing for was coming and we couldn't slow time down as much as we tried.

Her doctor spoke to us alone that Monday, he told us what we all had feared was happening. The antibiotics were not helping. They were also becoming too difficult to take, as Mum had stopped drinking as much as she had been just days earlier. He told us point-blank, 'Your mother has been fighting and she has done everything she can to try and hold on, and I am sorry to be the one to tell you this, but as of now your mother is starting to die. The dying process is now taking place.' He said it through glassy eyes.

As prepared as you think you are for anything in this world, you are never actually ready to hear the words, 'Your mother is dying.' You hear the words, and you know what they mean, this sadness overcomes you, but it's also not real, how can it be? How can the person you love more in this world than anyone, that you would do anything for, be leaving you behind? I was only 34, I needed my mum, as grown-up as I liked to think I was. I needed her to give me advice for the rest of my life, I needed to call her daily to hear her voice. My mum would never get to be a Baba. Even though we had been in hospital for two weeks to the day, we still had hope and we still prayed that Mum would be okay. I would never be ready to let her go, but we knew if we wanted Mum not to be in pain anymore, we would have to tell her it was okay to.

Meanwhile, in the outside world, things were changing, and we weren't even aware of them. We were living in a bubble, this bubble that consisted of us three kids spending every moment we had with Mum. When we weren't there, we were trying to organise things that would make Mum more comfortable or sorting out things, making arrangements for what happens next. I couldn't even remember the last time I thought about anything else, the days were a blur and I knew I had many people that cared about me and what was going on in my life at that moment, but I don't think I have ever felt so disconnected from reality.

One night we were crunching some numbers, making a plan of how to tackle the next part. We had no idea but were learning fast. Things were getting harder to face but we knew we were in it together. My sister was having a really hard time processing what was happening, so Michael and I took control of things related to finance. The truth was, Mum had no money. She had been living on her pension and the rest had gone towards her medical bills over the years. We were trying to calculate the costs and work out how we were going to cover everything. That night I got a video message from my mates at home, my Melbourne family, Brad, Mark, Lucy, Gav and Sylvia. I was so overwhelmed that I just started crying when I saw it come through. They were saying they wanted to do something to help. They knew we had been spending a lot of time and money with Mum and we hadn't been working, they knew Mike and I lived interstate with our partners who had been flying back and forth, so it all had to be adding up

– the accommodation, flights, on top of bills and funeral costs as well as a grave site. These were unthinkable things we had to work through daily, on our own. It was hell and then this video came through. They had set up a GoFundMe page to help raise money towards all costs. It was so thoughtful and so unexpected, we hadn't spoken a word to anyone about our financial worries. But they'd set all this up and donations had already hit over $5,000, just incredible! The generosity from people who'd donated, my family and friends from all parts of my life, some I hadn't spoken to in weeks or even years; this was just something else.

They had an idea and they put it in motion and it helped us out immensely; we will be forever grateful. Dealing with so much bad news, even for a positive person like me, it was hard to see the light, but the light was always there. It never went out and eternally I will remember that even in the darkest of hours, love means everything.

On Tuesday Mum slept most of the day. She managed to wake up a few times when she recognised someone's voice. Mum was very popular, and she'd been receiving a lot of visitors, but now we really had to limit them. Mum had too much pride and class, and we wanted her to be remembered as being just as stylish as she always had been. We sat around and chatted to her; even though Mum was often sleeping, the medical staff told us to continue to talk as she would hear us right until she left this world behind. Talked we did! We shared more tales and laughs; we knew sometimes she would hear us as a smirk or smile would come across her face. She looked peaceful and not to be in a great deal of pain.

That night it was my turn to stay. When any of us left for the night, we'd begun to say to Mum, 'We love you, we thank you and we have each other. We will love and care for and lean on each other, you can let go now.' It was strange to say, but Mum was just being so strong, we needed her to know it was okay to let go. We had been told earlier that week that the most important thing for someone in palliative care with a life-ending illness isn't the drugs or the food. The most important things are words.

Thank you.

I love you.

I forgive you.

Please forgive me.

We practised these lines religiously, we wanted Mum to know we meant them! Especially the words that would mean the most to her, 'I love you and I thank you.' Now, you might be thinking, if these are the words I said to my mother, what is the last thing Mum said to me? I would like to tell you it was something deep, some life advice that I could forever remember and think, yes Mum, I will do those things for you, always and forever.

I was with my brother walking him down to the car. He turned around with a big smile on his face and told me Mum just did the cutest thing as he was saying goodnight. He told her he loved her and thanked her, and she told him that she loved him. She said the words and that makes all this worth it. Just to hear your mum say those three little words.

I started laughing and couldn't really stop. What the fuck, how did he get such a sweet farewell? I was only just behind him saying goodnight and do you want to know what she said to me?

'Mumma, you know I thank you for everything you do, you are the world's best mum,' I gleam.

Mum nods and smiles.

'Mumma, you know I love you so very much!' I add.

Mum nods and this time goes to add something, and she hadn't really spoken all day, so I lean in to listen closely.

'Okay, Darling, but can you get off me now as you're covering me in mincemeat!'

Yep, that's what I got. I got mincemeat! You have to laugh! I knew Mum loved me and I didn't need to hear it. Well, that's what I tell myself.

That night I cried to Mum again, told her all the things I had wanted to tell her just days earlier but didn't have the strength to. I spoke to her about funeral arrangements, but by then she was not responding.

'Mumma, if you are too stubborn to have this chat with me, like all the other times I've tried before, you are just going to have to hear what I have to say. Ideally, I would have liked your advice or opinion, but here we are,' I would tease.

The next morning I also read her the speech I had been preparing to read at her service. That sounds strange, I know, but I actually found it calming to write while I was by my mum's side because I could look up and see her peaceful there and my heart felt full and the love I had for her was so strong; even when you don't think you can love someone more, you can.

Wednesday was the hardest of them all. Mum had not woken up, she had not eaten or drunk a thing and we could feel the end was close. We held on to her, like she held on to us.

We didn't want to leave her, and yet we knew we had to. We spent the day looking through photos and talking, laughing and crying. My brother was on duty that night but geez, I couldn't leave. I couldn't leave if I tried. I mean, you always got the fear when you were leaving. Especially when it was nightfall, that's when those dark thoughts came to mind. I knew I told Mum she could let go, but could I? I stayed till late, I just wasn't ready to go.

We had been told by the doctor, it's hard to say when. They can't give you an exact time frame, they just tell you it's happening. We also got told, as much as you try to be there 24/7, and with your loved ones for their final moments, there could be a chance they go when you have stepped out of the room to grab something to eat or make a phone call or use the bathroom. His advice was, don't be hard on yourselves if you miss it, and sometimes, people wait for that moment, so you don't have the burden of experiencing it. I knew this, but couldn't help how I felt. I was my mum's lifeguard, security guard, I was her best mate.

It got so late that my brother said, 'Let's pop out, let's give Mum 15 minutes to herself and then if you want to stay you can. I can't tell you what to decide.' We popped out and spoke about everything, life, Mum, it's all a blur. When we came back in, Mum was peacefully sleeping. I knew it was time to go home. My brother promised he would call if anything happened overnight.

The next morning, Thursday, 12 March 2020, I got there early, just to be there by her side. We all just sat around. It's a strange feeling waiting for someone you love to die, the signs were there,

there wasn't any waking up, her breathing had changed, she wasn't moving. The moment we were dreading in our guts was coming. Time goes on and moments pass, and life is just brought down to these final moments that don't feel real, it doesn't matter what you think you have or haven't achieved in life, in those final moments, nothing matters but love. The love that can be felt through anything, any moment, distance or situation in time – that is what it all comes down to.

Nada, Mum's soul sister, was back, with her daughter Kate who's a medical professional and also loved my mother dearly. They had brought us coffees and it was a beautiful sunny day, so we decided to enjoy them outside. We needed to give Mum a break. We had Mum's window open so the room could feel the breeze and sunlight was peering through. It was about 2pm, the days had blurred together, I hadn't been at work for three weeks this time round. Mike mentioned to Mum that we were stepping out for some sun, and that we loved her. Dana spent a few more moments with Mum and when she came to join us, she was sobbing. She was heartbroken, she had a terrible feeling that it was happening. The feeling that comes with this whole experience is strange, like time is slowed down, but then sped up. We must have sat outside for about 20 minutes, the talking and laughter coming from a sleep-deprived not to mention emotional bunch, I know Mum would have heard the laughter and tales through the open window.

I popped to the bathroom before I went back in, Dana following close behind while Michael headed straight back to the room. As he did, a nurse was just leaving. She said she had checked on Mum and she was still breathing, it was just time for her injection for pain relief. My brother walked into the room and he knew in that moment Mum was gone. She must have had her last breath as he was entering the room. He looked up at me as I entered moments later, a look of heartache on his face. Before Dana and Michael said anything, I too knew just from the feeling in the room and the looks of despair.

Mum had left this world behind; her courageous six-year battle with breast cancer was over. She fought till the very last breath and of course being the world's most stubborn woman waited until all three kids were there together as one, but also for when we weren't in the room with her as she didn't want to leave that final moment with us. Mum was still protecting us till the very last breath. All my life I had feared this moment, the moment my mum would be gone, but she finally looked in peace. Writing this breaks my heart all over again and the tears never seem to end.

I know in my heart of hearts, my mother, a woman of so much style and grace, felt the love, felt all the love around her right until her last breath. She knew she had been an incredible mother; she had raised us all to our full potential despite the hardships she faced her whole life, the let-downs and the battles. She never once became a victim. She refused to let life paint her with that brush it so heavy-handedly tried to stroke her with time and time again. She knew she was our rock and our hero, and I know she's looking down on us right now knowing she did do the best damn job she could, and we will forever be thankful and love her for that. Love is endless and knows no boundaries.

EPILOGUE

Mum passed away eight days before the government restricted hospital visitors to two people for one hour per day all around Australia, as well as only allowing 10 people to attend a funeral due to COVID-19.

Our mum's service had close to 200 people and even though we respected the Serbian Orthodox traditional church service and funeral, the wake was a celebration of Mum's life with all her favourite people and all her most loved songs.

I read my eulogy as planned and felt this calmness as my siblings and husband stood behind me – I could feel their hands on my back supporting me, giving me the courage and strength I needed to speak on behalf of the three of us kids. I know in my heart that Mum was looking down, she is with me every day of my life, and even though I can't call her on the phone, I speak to her daily and let her know how much I love her and miss her.

One of the greatest gifts in the world is love.

To love, to feel loved and to experience love.

I now also know one of the greatest compliments I can get in this world is when someone looks at me or speaks to me and says the words, 'God, you're like your mother!'

I will forever hold Mum close in my heart and live life not as a victim but as a woman of pride and positivity because life is what you make it and you only get one chance, so be the best you can and keep your head up high – you will empower others to do so too.

ACKNOWLEDGEMENTS

There are some very important people that helped this book come to life. It would not have been possible without their guidance and encouragement.

Firstly, to my brother Michael, who has motivated me from day one to put my idea into action. He believed in me, told me I had a story to tell and supported me through the writing process. There were too many phone calls and text messages to count. Thank you for your constant encouragement. You pushed me to speak the truth and tell my story and revel in the process.

To my sister Dana, the creative genius behind the artwork and design of the book. Late-night phone calls and emails, brainstorming, going back and forth with design suggestions until she had a brilliant idea – to use my childlike handwriting on the cover to introduce my story. Although somewhat more hesitant about this story being told, you told me this is our past and it has made us who we are today, and accepted it was something I had to do. Thank you.

To my husband Johannes, who looks at me every day like I am Superwoman, the love and support he gives me every day of our lives is endless. He told me I have a talent and have always been a good storyteller, and even though my readers now know about that one time he accidentally shaved his eyebrows off, he still loves me. That's when you know you are onto a very supportive partner. Thank you, Lover Boy.

To my editor Des, who mentored me during this process. I came to her with what I thought might have been a silly idea, a big dream and with no idea how to get there. She told me that my goddess Mumma shines through my story, my style of writing was perfect and thanked me for trusting her with my words and story. From that moment I knew I was going to really do it! Write a book! A bucket-list thing became a reality and without her guidance and feedback, this wouldn't have been possible. Des, you encouraged me to do my best. For that I am forever grateful.

To my publisher Blaise at Busybird Publishing, who guided me through the publication process in such a professional yet down-to-earth way. Nothing seemed too overwhelming and her calm approach assured me I didn't need to worry about a thing. Thank you.

To my friends, who know who they are, the people in my life that motivate me every day. From my childhood, through the years and more recently, there are too many of them to list. Some I haven't seen for years and some I speak to every day. My friends are what make me whole and who make me want to get up every day, to be a better person. My friends are my family! Thanks for the laughs, good times, beers and also the tears.

To the rest of my family, who know I love them, they have always been a huge part of my life. Family means the world to me! I am grateful for the love you give me every day. To my Kumovi, an extra special shout-out to you all. Thank you for always being there when we need you.

Finally, to my beautiful mother, Olga. Mum, I would never have done this if not for you – you are my inspiration. I would have been too scared and too nervous, but wow Chookie, you have showed me what courage is. You were the bravest person I knew, and you always kept your head up high. The love you gave me was beyond doubt the greatest gift anyone has ever given me. Thank you for being my hero!

CPSIA information can be obtained
at www.ICGtesting.com
Printed in the USA
BVHW031351181021
619199BV00009B/340